EASY
CHINESE
& FAR EASTERN
COOKING

EASY CHINESE & FAR EASTERN COOKING

Ho Mei Yin

Larousse & Co., Inc., New York

© Ward Lock Limited 1985

Illustrations © Orbis-Verlag für Publizistik 1985 and
Hitgeverij Het Spectrum B.V., De Meern, Netherlands 1985

First published in the United States and Canada by
Larousse & Co., Inc.,
572 Fifth Avenue, New York, N.Y. 10036

ISBN 0-88332-458-X

Printed and bound in Spain by Graficromo, S.A., Cordoba

Notes

It is important to follow *either* the metric, imperial *or* American measures when using the recipes in this book. Do not use a combination of measures.

American terminology within recipes is indicated by the use of brackets in both the list of ingredients and in the methods.

American measures which follow metric and imperial measures within the recipe methods are preceded by the term 'US'.

All spoon measures are level.

Each dish will serve four people, unless indicated otherwise.

Flour is plain (all-purpose) and sugar is granulated, unless indicated otherwise.

Unusual ingredients may be purchased from Chinese supermarkets and other Oriental food shops.

CONTENTS

SOUPS

Basic Chicken Stock

Metric/imperial		American
1.5kg/3 lb	boiling chicken, quartered	3 lb
2 litres/ 3½ pints	water	2 quarts
	1 small onion, chopped	
	3 sticks celery, chopped	
	1 small piece root ginger, crushed	
1 × 15ml spoon/ 1 tablespoon	dry sherry	1 tablespoon
1 × 5ml spoon/ 1 teaspoon	salt	1 teaspoon

Place the chicken pieces in a large, heavy saucepan. Add the water and bring to the boil. Skim off any froth or bits which rise to the surface. Reduce the heat and simmer, covered, for 1½ hours.

Remove the chicken pieces from the pan and discard; all their flavour will have cooked out. Add the onion, celery and ginger to the stock and allow to stand for 20 minutes. Then add the sherry and salt and simmer for 10 minutes. Strain the stock through a clean cloth, leave to cool completely, then skim off the fat which will have risen to the surface.

Hun-t'un-t'ang

(Wonton Soup)

SERVES 6

Metric/imperial		American
100g/4 oz	flour	1 cup
	salt	
	1 egg	
1 × 15ml spoon/ 1 tablespoon	milk	1 tablespoon
2 × 15ml spoons/ 2 tablespoons	oil	2 tablespoons
100g/4 oz	spinach, washed and picked over	¼ lb
100g/4 oz	minced (ground) pork	¼ lb
2 × 5ml spoons/ 2 teaspoons	soy sauce	2 teaspoons
	ground ginger	
1.5 litres/ 2½ pints	chicken stock	1¾ quarts
1 × 15ml spoon/ 1 tablespoon	chopped chives	1 tablespoon

Wontons are small, stuffed pastry parcels; they are usually eaten as an accompaniment to soup.

To make the wontons, sift the flour and a pinch of salt into a bowl. Break in the egg and add the milk and oil. Mix to a firm but pliant dough. Roll out very thinly on a lightly floured surface. Cut into 7.5cm/3 inch squares. Cover with a cloth while preparing the stuffing.

To make the stuffing, put the spinach into a bowl, pour boiling water over and leave for 3 minutes. Drain well and chop. Put the pork in a bowl and stir in the soy sauce and a pinch of ground ginger. Add the spinach and mix.

Put 1 × 5ml spoon/1 teaspoon of stuffing in the centre of each pastry square. Fold over one side of the pastry to form a roll, pressing to seal the long edge. Fold the two ends of pastry at the ends of the roll over each other and press together. Bring the stock to the boil in a large saucepan. Add the wontons and simmer, covered, for 20 minutes. Divide the wontons into soup bowls and pour the stock over them. Sprinkle with chives and serve.

Basic Meat Stock

Metric/imperial		American
450g/1 lb	lean pork	1 lb
250g/9 oz	chicken wings, carcass, giblets, etc.	generous ½ lb
2 litres/ 3½ pints	water	2 quarts
	2 carrots, chopped	
	1 small onion, chopped	
	1 piece root ginger, crushed	
1 × 5ml spoon/ 1 teaspoon	salt	1 teaspoon
2 × 5ml spoons/ 2 teaspoons	soy sauce	2 teaspoons

Place the pork and chicken in a large, heavy saucepan. Add the water and bring slowly to the boil. Skim off any froth or bits which rise to the surface. Reduce the heat and simmer, covered, for 20 minutes. Remove the pork and chicken from the pan; they can be kept for other dishes. Add the carrots, onion and ginger to the stock and simmer for 30 minutes. Add the salt and soy sauce and simmer for a further 5 minutes. Strain the stock through a clean cloth, leave to cool completely, then skim off the fat which will have risen to the surface.

Chinese Noodle Soup

SERVES 6

Metric/imperial		American
200g/7 oz	boneless leg of pork	scant ½ lb
2 × 15ml spoons/ 2 tablespoons	Chinese rice wine or dry sherry	2 tablespoons
2 × 15ml spoons/ 2 tablespoons	soy sauce	2 tablespoons
	salt, pepper, ground ginger	
15g/½ oz	dried Chinese mushrooms	¾ cup
150g/5 oz	bamboo shoots	1 cup
100g/4 oz	cooked chicken	¾ cup
100g/4 oz	cooked ham, sliced	¼ lb
250g/9 oz	transparent noodles	generous ½ lb
2 litres/ 3½ pints	chicken stock (page 6)	2 quarts
	oil for frying	
	cress	

Cut the pork into small strips. Mix the rice wine or sherry, soy sauce and seasonings to taste in a bowl. Add the pork, cover and leave to marinate for 1 hour. After 30 minutes put the mushrooms to soak in warm water for 15–30 minutes, until swollen. Meanwhile, prepare the other ingredients. Cut the bamboo shoots into thin strips and cut the chicken into 2.5 cm/1 inch cubes. Trim any fat from the ham and cut into 2.5 cm/1 inch squares. Bring a pan of salted water to the boil. Add the noodles and simmer for 10 minutes. Drain in a sieve, rinse in cold water and drain again. Drain the mushrooms.

Put the stock, mushrooms, bamboo shoots and noodles into a large saucepan. Heat gently for 3 minutes. Meanwhile take the pork out of the marinade and drain. Heat the oil in a frying pan and fry the pork strips on all sides for 2 minutes. Remove and add to the soup with the chicken and ham pieces. Heat through gently. Pour the soup into warmed soup bowls, sprinkle with cress and serve.

Chinese Noodle Soup

Chinese Pork and Bean Sprout Soup

Metric/imperial		American
20g/¾ oz	dried Chinese mushrooms	1 cup
50g/2 oz	transparent noodles	2 oz
300g/11 oz	lean pork	scant ¾ lb
50ml/2 fl oz	oil	¼ cup
	1 onion, chopped	
	1 clove garlic, chopped	
150g/5 oz	bean sprouts	1½ cups
1.5 litres/ 2½ pints	hot chicken stock (page 6)	1¾ quarts
	salt, pepper	
2 × 15ml spoons/ 2 tablespoons	soy sauce	2 tablespoons
	sugar	

Soak the mushrooms in warm water for 15–30 minutes, until swollen. Cut the noodles into 10cm/4 inch lengths. Put them into a bowl and cover with boiling salted water. Allow to stand for 5 minutes. Drain, rinse with cold water and drain again. Drain the mushrooms, and halve or quarter them if large. While the mushrooms and noodles are soaking, cut the pork into narrow strips.

Heat the oil in a pan and fry the pork on all sides for 5 minutes. Remove and keep hot. Fry the onion and garlic in the pan for 3 minutes, until just soft. Put the pork back in the pan, and add the bean sprouts, noodles, mushrooms and stock. Season with salt, pepper, the soy sauce and a pinch of sugar. Bring to the boil and simmer for 8 minutes. Serve in warmed soup bowls.

Kiemblo

(Chinese Soup with Vegetables, Beef and Dumplings)

Metric/imperial		American
	1 slice wholemeal (wholewheat) bread, crusts removed	
250g/9 oz	minced (ground) beef	generous ½ lb
	salt, pepper	
1.5 litres/ 2½ pints	meat stock (page 7)	1¾ quarts
1 × 15ml spoon/ 1 tablespoon	oil	1 tablespoon
	1 onion, sliced	
150g/5 oz	savoy cabbage, chopped	1¾ cups
	1 leek, sliced	
50g/2 oz	fresh mushrooms, sliced	¾ cup
175g/6 oz	celery, sliced	1½ cups
50g/2 oz	peas	⅓ cup
100g/4 oz	ribbon noodles	¼ lb
1 × 15ml spoon/ 1 tablespoon	soy sauce	1 tablespoon
3 × 15ml spoons/ 3 tablespoons	Chinese rice wine or dry sherry	3 tablespoons

Soak the bread in a little water and squeeze out the excess. Mix the beef and bread together and season to taste. Shape into small oval dumplings with a teaspoon. Bring the stock to the boil in a pan, put in the dumplings, and simmer for 10 minutes. Meanwhile heat the oil in a large saucepan, add the onion, and fry for 3 minutes until pale brown. Add the cabbage, leek, mushrooms and celery and fry for another 5 minutes. Take the dumplings out of the stock, drain and keep warm. Strain the stock on to the vegetable mixture. Add the peas and noodles and simmer for 15 minutes, until the peas and noodles are done. Put the dumplings back into the soup, add the soy sauce and rice wine or sherry, and season to taste. Serve at once.

Kiemblo

Soto Ajam

Soto Ajam

(Indonesian Chicken Soup)

Metric/imperial		American
2 litres/ 3½ pints	salted water	2 quarts
1.5kg/3 lb	boiling chicken	3 lb
	1 small onion, sliced	
	5 cloves garlic, sliced	
1 × 15ml spoon/ 1 tablespoon	ground ginger	1 tablespoon
	pepper	
200g/7 oz	bean sprouts	2 cups
225g/8 oz	cooked celery, chopped	1½ cups
100ml/4 fl oz	dry sherry	½ cup
	soy sauce	
	4 hard-boiled eggs, chopped	
1 × 15ml spoon/ 1 tablespoon	chopped chives	1 tablespoon

Bring the water to the boil in a large pan. Put in the chicken, cover and simmer for 1 hour, or until tender.

Remove the chicken from the stock and put aside. Add the onion, garlic, ginger, and pepper to taste to the stock and simmer for 15 minutes. Meanwhile remove the skin from the chicken, take the meat off the bones and cut into small, even sized pieces. Keep warm. Mix the bean sprouts and celery in a bowl with the sherry. Season to taste with soy sauce. Put the chicken pieces into a warmed soup tureen, add the vegetables and eggs, and pour the stock on top. Sprinkle with chives and serve.

Chinese Vegetable Soup

Metric/imperial		American
250g/9 oz	lean pork	generous ½ lb
5 × 15ml spoons/ 5 tablespoons	soy sauce	⅓ cup
2 × 5ml spoons/ 2 teaspoons	flour	2 teaspoons
	salt, pepper, ground ginger	
	2 carrots, peeled	
100g/4 oz	bamboo shoots	¾ cup
50g/2 oz	spinach, washed and picked over	1 cup
2 × 15ml spoons/ 2 tablespoons	oil	2 tablespoons
1.5 litres/ 2½ pints	meat stock (page 7)	1¾ quarts
50g/2 oz	fresh mushrooms, thinly sliced	¾ cup
15g/½ oz	transparent noodles	½ oz
2 × 15ml spoons/ 2 tablespoons	Chinese rice wine or dry sherry	2 tablespoons

Cut the pork into narrow strips. Mix 2 × 15ml spoons/ 2 tablespoons soy sauce with the flour in a cup. Season to taste with salt and pepper. Put the meat in a bowl, spoon the marinade over it, cover and leave to stand for 10 minutes. Meanwhile cut the carrots and bamboo shoots into thin strips. Cut the spinach leaves in half.

Heat the oil in a large saucepan. Remove the meat from the marinade, drain and fry in the oil, on all sides, for 10 minutes. Add the stock to the pan with the carrots and simmer for another 10 minutes. Add the bamboo shoots, mushrooms and noodles and simmer for a further 10 minutes, until just tender. Five minutes before the end of the cooking time add the spinach leaves. Season to taste with the remaining soy sauce, the rice wine or sherry, ginger and salt. Serve at once in warmed soup bowls.

Vietnamese Abalone Soup

Metric/imperial		American
1 litre/1¾ pints	good clear stock (see **Note**)	1 quart
90g/3½ oz	long-grain rice	½ cup
175g/6 oz	canned abalone	6 oz
2 × 15ml spoons/ 2 tablespoons	oil	2 tablespoons
	1 onion, chopped	
	1 clove garlic, crushed	
	salt, pepper, allspice	
	1 sprig tarragon, chopped	

Bring the stock to the boil in a large saucepan. Add the rice and boil for 15 minutes until tender. Meanwhile, drain the abalone, reserving the liquid, and cut the shellfish into strips. Heat the oil in a frying pan, add the onion, and fry until lightly browned. Add the abalone and garlic, cook gently for a few minutes, then add to the rice-stock mixture with the reserved abalone liquid. Re-heat and add the seasonings to taste. Serve the soup in warmed soup bowls, and sprinkle the tarragon over the top.

Note If you have no good stock available, use canned consommé or a stock cube.

Hay Hong Lo Soen

(Chinese Asparagus Soup)

Metric/imperial		American
900ml/1½ pints	chicken stock (page 6)	1 quart
150g/5 oz	leeks, sliced	generous ¼ lb
	1 clove garlic	
	salt, pepper, ground ginger, curry powder	
1 × 15ml spoon/ 1 tablespoon	dripping or chicken fat	1 tablespoon
2 × 15ml spoons/ 2 tablespoons	soy sauce	2 tablespoons
175g/6 oz	crabmeat	1 cup
250g/9 oz	asparagus spears, cooked	generous ½ lb

Bring the chicken stock to the boil in a large saucepan, add the leeks and simmer for 20 minutes. Crush the garlic with salt. Melt the dripping or chicken fat in another pan and fry the garlic until golden. Add to the soup, then add the soy sauce and seasonings to taste. Remove any hard pieces from the crabmeat, flake it and add to the soup. Add the asparagus spears, then heat them in the soup. Adjust seasoning and serve.

FIRST COURSES, SAUCES AND SIDE DISHES

Spring Rolls

Metric/imperial		American
250g/9 oz	flour	2¼ cups
350ml/12 fl oz	water	1½ cups
1½ × 5ml spoons/ 1½ teaspoons	groundnut (peanut) oil	1½ teaspoons
	salt, cayenne pepper	
50ml/2 fl oz	oil	¼ cup
125g/4½ oz	minced (ground) pork	¼ lb
125g/4½ oz	minced (ground) beef	¼ lb
250g/9 oz	white or Chinese cabbage, shredded	3 cups
	1 leek, cut into thin strips	
	1 onion, finely chopped	
225g/8 oz	bamboo shoots, cut into thin strips	1½ cups
100g/4 oz	mushrooms, chopped	1½ cups
200g/7 oz	bean sprouts	2 cups
50ml/2 fl oz	soy sauce	¼ cup
50ml/2 fl oz	Chinese rice wine or dry sherry	¼ cup
	groundnut (peanut) oil for frying	
	1 egg yolk, beaten	
	oil for deep frying	

First make the batter. Place the flour in a bowl and gradually stir in the water, stirring in the same direction all the time. Stir in the groundnut (peanut) oil and a pinch of salt. Cover and leave to stand for 30 minutes.

To prepare the stuffing, heat the oil in a pan. Add the minced (ground) meats and fry for 2 minutes, stirring. Add the cabbage, leek, onion and bamboo shoots, and fry gently for 5 minutes. Add the mushrooms and bean sprouts, and stew for a further 2 minutes. Season with the soy sauce, rice wine or sherry, salt and cayenne pepper. Set aside.

Lightly paint the surface of a large frying pan with groundnut (peanut) oil. Pour in an eighth of the batter, spread it out evenly by tilting the pan, and cook over a very gentle heat until firm and lightly browned on both sides. Make 7 other pancakes in the same way, placing them between damp tea towels when cooked.

Cut the 8 pancakes into 8 large squares. Divide the stuffing between the pancakes, spreading it out on the surface. Fold two opposite corners towards the middle. Starting with one of the other corners (the one nearest to you) roll up the pancake. Paint the last corner with beaten egg yolk and press the roll well together. Heat the oil to a temperature of 180°C/350°F and deep fry the spring rolls. Take them out, drain on absorbent paper and serve on a warmed dish.

Sweet-and-sour Sauce

Metric/imperial		American
20g/¾ oz	cornflour (cornstarch)	3 tablespoons
100ml/4 fl oz	water	½ cup
40g/1½ oz	soft brown sugar	2½ tablespoons
150ml/¼ pint	red wine	⅔ cup
3 × 15ml spoons/ 3 tablespoons	tomato ketchup	3 tablespoons
1 × 15ml spoon/ 1 tablespoon	soy sauce	1 tablespoon
1 × 5ml spoon/ 1 teaspoon	mustard powder	1 teaspoon
	1 green pepper, de-seeded and finely chopped	
	1 large, firm tomato, de-seeded and finely chopped	
	3 slices canned pineapple, finely chopped	
	salt, pepper	

Mix together the cornflour (cornstarch) and water in a pan until smooth. Add the sugar, wine, tomato ketchup, soy sauce and mustard powder. Bring slowly to the boil, stirring continuously. Boil for 2 minutes, until the sauce turns clear, then add the pepper, tomato and pineapple. Bring the sauce back to the boil and adjust seasoning to taste. Serve in a warmed sauceboat.

Sambal Goreng Hati

(Liver Sambal)

Metric/imperial		American
250–300g/9–11 oz	calves' liver	generous $\frac{1}{2}$–$\frac{3}{4}$ lb
	1 small onion, chopped	
	1 clove garlic, crushed	
$1\frac{1}{2}$ × 5ml spoons/ $1\frac{1}{2}$ teaspoons	chilli sauce	$1\frac{1}{2}$ teaspoons
1 × 5ml spoon/ 1 teaspoon	soft brown sugar	1 teaspoon
1 × 2.5ml spoon/ $\frac{1}{2}$ teaspoon	belacan (prawn paste)	$\frac{1}{2}$ teaspoon
1 × 5ml spoon/ 1 teaspoon	salt	1 teaspoon
3 × 15ml spoons/ 3 tablespoons	oil	3 tablespoons
1 × 15ml spoon/ 1 tablespoon	tamarind pulp, chopped	1 tablespoon
225ml/7 fl oz	coconut milk	1 cup

Soak the liver in cold water for 15 minutes. Remove from the water, pat dry with absorbent paper, and cut into short, thin strips. Pound and mash together the onion, garlic, chilli sauce, sugar, belacan (prawn paste) and salt. Heat the oil in a heavy-based pan and fry the mixture. Add the liver and continue frying over medium heat, turning occasionally, until the liver starts to brown. Add the tamarind and stir for 1 minute. Pour in the coconut milk and allow to simmer for 5 minutes. Serve as a side dish with a Malaysian or Indonesian-style meal.

Peacock Platter

The peacock platter is a cold Chinese hors d'oeuvre consisting of thinly sliced meats and other ingredients, and it is served on special occasions. If prepared and arranged with care, the dish looks like the outspread tail of a displaying peacock. It is impossible to give an exact recipe: it can be as simple or as elaborate as you like. Among possible ingredients are: boiled or steamed chicken, red-cooked meat or poultry, ham and abalone. All ingredients are very thinly sliced and then arranged in the form of a fan on a flat dish.

As can be seen from the picture, slices of hard-boiled eggs, decorated with red and green cocktail cherries, can be used to represent the eyes of the peacock. Other decoration can be provided by figures cut out of carrots or radishes. Asparagus, cucumber slices, radish roses, pieces of pineapple, and anything else you like can be used to decorate the peacock's tail. Hoisin and plum sauce can be served as dips, and can be bought ready-prepared from oriental food shops.

Sambal Bajak

(Hot Sauce)

Metric/imperial		American
	8–10 red chilli peppers, de-seeded and finely chopped	
	4–6 red onions, chopped	
	2 cloves garlic, crushed	
	8 blanched almonds, crushed	
1 × 5ml spoon/ 1 teaspoon	belacan (prawn paste)	1 teaspoon
1 × 15ml spoon/ 1 tablespoon	soft brown sugar	1 tablespoon
1 × 5ml spoon/ 1 teaspoon	salt	1 teaspoon
2 × 15ml spoons/ 2 tablespoons	oil	2 tablespoons
2 × 15ml spoons/ 2 tablespoons	tamarind pulp, chopped	2 tablespoons
	1 bay leaf	
2 × 15ml spoons/ 2 tablespoons	water	2 tablespoons

Thoroughly pound and mash together the chillies, onions, garlic, nuts, belacan (prawn paste), sugar and salt. Heat the oil in a heavy-based pan and fry the spice mixture in it for 2 to 3 minutes. Add the tamarind, bay leaf and water, and continue simmering over medium heat until all the oil has been absorbed. Stir continuously to prevent sticking, especially as the ingredients become drier. Remove the bay leaf, let the sambal cool to room temperature, and then transfer to a clean glass jar. Store tightly covered, in the refrigerator.

Peacock Platter

Sambal Taoco

(Soya Bean Hot Sauce)

Metric/imperial		American
	8–10 red chilli peppers, de-seeded and finely chopped	
	3–4 red onions, chopped	
	3 cloves garlic, crushed	
1 × 2.5ml spoon/ ½ teaspoon	belacan (prawn paste)	½ teaspoon
1 × 5ml spoon/ 1 teaspoon	soft brown sugar	1 teaspoon
2–3 × 15ml spoons/ 2–3 tablespoons	oil	2–3 tablespoons
3–4 × 15ml spoons/ 3–4 tablespoons	soya bean paste	3–4 tablespoons
1 × 15ml spoon/ 1 tablespoon	tamarind pulp, chopped	1 tablespoon
3–4 × 15ml spoons/ 3–4 tablespoons	water	3–4 tablespoons

Thoroughly pound and mash together the chillies, onions, garlic, belacan (prawn paste) and sugar. Heat the oil in a heavy-based pan, add the spice mixture and fry for 2 to 3 minutes. Add the soya bean paste, tamarind and water and simmer gently until all the oil has been absorbed. Let the sambal cool to room temperature, and then transfer to a clean glass jar. Store tightly covered, in the refrigerator.

Rempeyek Ikan Teri

(Dried Fish Pancakes)

Metric/imperial		American
	2 cloves garlic, crushed	
1 × 2.5ml spoon/ ½ teaspoon	ground coriander	½ teaspoon
1 × 2.5ml spoon/ ½ teaspoon	turmeric	½ teaspoon
	3 blanched almonds, mashed	
	salt	
3–5 × 15ml spoons/ 3–5 tablespoons	coconut milk	3–5 tablespoons
100g/4 oz	rice flour	¾ cup
25g/1 oz	dried ikan teri or canned anchovies (see **Note**)	1 oz
	oil for frying	

Pound and mash together the garlic, coriander, turmeric, nuts and a pinch of salt. Stir sufficient coconut milk into the flour to make a smooth batter, not too thin. Stir the fish and the spice mixture into the batter, and leave to stand for 10 minutes. Heat a film of oil in a wok or frying pan. Stir the batter again, put a spoonful into the pan and tip so that it quickly spreads to cover the base of the pan. Fry to a golden brown on both sides, remove from the pan and drain on absorbent paper. Keep warm. Continue until all the batter has been cooked. Serve as a side dish with a Malaysian or Indonesian-style meal.

Note Ikan teri are tiny, anchovy-like dried fish that can be eaten whole, although some people prefer to snap the heads off first. These dried fish are sold in oriental food shops, sometimes curried. When the fish are to be fried, as in this recipe, it is advisable to dry them out a little more, either in the sun, or indoors near the fire or a radiator. (Canned anchovies will, of course, need drying completely.)

Sambal Goreng Telur

(Egg Sambal)

Metric/imperial		American
	3 red chilli peppers, de-seeded and finely chopped	
	4 red onions, chopped	
	2 cloves garlic, crushed	
1 × 2.5ml spoon/ ½ teaspoon	belacan (prawn paste)	½ teaspoon
2 × 5ml spoons/ 2 teaspoons	ground galingale (optional)	2 teaspoons
1 × 15ml spoon/ 1 tablespoon	soft brown sugar	1 tablespoon
1 × 15ml spoon/ 1 tablespoon	tamarind pulp, chopped	1 tablespoon
	salt	
2 × 15ml spoons/ 2 tablespoons	oil	2 tablespoons
250ml/8 fl oz	coconut milk	1 cup
	2 bay leaves	
	4 hard-boiled eggs	

Pound and mash together the chillies, onions, garlic, belacan (prawn paste), galingale, brown sugar and tamarind. Season to taste with salt. Heat the oil in a heavy-based pan, add the mashed ingredients and fry gently for 2 to 3 minutes. Add the coconut milk and bay leaves, stir, and simmer for a few minutes. Add the eggs and simmer gently, stirring occasionally, until the oil separates from the sauce. Remove the eggs from the pan, let them cool a little, and halve them lengthways. Place them on a dish with the rounded side uppermost. Pour the sauce over and serve immediately as a hot side dish with a Malaysian or Indonesian-style dinner.

FISH AND SHELLFISH

Uwo no Amazukake

(Japanese Fish in Sweet-and-sour Sauce)

Metric/imperial		American
600g/1¼ lb	fillets of white fish	1¼ lb
	juice of ½ lemon	
5 × 15ml spoons/ 5 tablespoons	soy sauce	⅓ cup
	salt	
25g/1 oz	potato flour	3 tablespoons
5 × 15ml spoons/ 5 tablespoons	vinegar	5 tablespoons
150ml/¼ pint	water	⅔ cup
25g/1 oz	sugar	2 tablespoons
	3 slices lemon	
	oil for deep frying	
25g/1 oz	cornflour (cornstarch)	¼ cup

Wash the fish fillets under the cold tap and pat dry with absorbent paper. Put them in a bowl and trickle the lemon juice over. Add 2 × 15ml spoons/2 tablespoons soy sauce. Turn the fish in the marinade, then cut into strips 3 cm/1¼ inches wide. Leave to marinate for 15 minutes. Season with salt and toss in the potato flour. Form the strips of fish into sausage shapes with your hands.

To make the sauce, put the vinegar, water, sugar, remaining soy sauce and the lemon slices in a pan. Bring to the boil, then reduce the heat and simmer very gently for 20 minutes. Meanwhile, deep fry the fish in the oil for about 8 minutes. Remove from the oil, drain on absorbent paper and keep warm. Finally, thicken the sauce. Mix the cornflour (cornstarch) to a smooth paste in a cup with a little cold water. Blend a little of the hot sauce into the mixture, then return to the pan. Bring slowly to the boil, stirring constantly. Simmer for 2–3 minutes to allow the flour to cook through.

To serve, arrange the fish on a warmed dish. The sauce can either be poured over, or served separately in a sauceboat.

Ten Tijun Yu

(Chinese Fish)

Metric/imperial		American
400g/14 oz	whole trout, cleaned	scant 1 lb
1.5kg/3 lb	whole carp, cleaned	3 lb
	juice of 1½ lemons	
	salt, pepper, ground star anise	
50g/2 oz	smoked ham	2 oz
450g/1 lb	fresh mushrooms, sliced	1 lb
	2 pieces preserved stem ginger, sliced	
3 × 15ml spoons/ 3 tablespoons	soy sauce	3 tablespoons
300ml/½ pint	hot water	1¼ cups
	4 large savoy cabbage leaves	
2 × 5ml spoons/ 2 teaspoons	cornflour (cornstarch)	2 teaspoons
40g/1½ oz	pork or bacon dripping	3 tablespoons
1 × 15ml spoon/ 1 tablespoon	chopped parsley	1 tablespoon
	1 lemon, sliced	

Wash both fish under the cold tap and pat dry with absorbent paper. Season inside and out with the juice of 1 lemon. Make several cuts across the backs of both fish. Rub in salt and pepper. Cut the ham into thin strips and insert into the cuts. Grease an oval ovenproof dish and put the fish in it. Mix together the mushrooms and ginger and scatter over the fish. Pour the soy sauce over and sprinkle with a pinch of ground star anise. Add a little of the hot water, cover and place in the oven. Bake for 30 minutes at 200°C/400°F/Gas 6.

While the fish is baking, add the rest of the hot water gradually. Baste the fish from time to time with the cooking liquid. Remove when cooked and arrange on the cabbage leaves in a warmed dish. Keep warm.

Stir the fish juices from the baking dish with a little cold water and bring to the boil. To thicken the sauce, mix the cornflour (cornstarch) to a smooth paste in a cup with a little cold water. Blend a little of the hot liquid into the mixture, then return to the baking dish. Bring slowly to the boil, stirring constantly. Simmer for 2–3 minutes to allow the flour to cook through. Pour into a sauceboat to serve separately and keep warm. Heat the dripping and pour over the fish with the juice of ½ lemon. Garnish with the parsley and lemon slices and serve with the sauce.

Oriental Fish with Grapefruit

Metric/imperial		American
750g/1¾ lb	**fillet of cod in one piece**	1¾ lb
	1 grapefruit, halved	
25g/1 oz	**butter**	2 tablespoons
	1 small onion, chopped	
25g/1 oz	**flour**	¼ cup
300ml/½ pint	**double (heavy) cream**	1¼ cups
	salt, pepper, ground ginger	
	2 hard-boiled eggs, chopped	
	COURT BOUILLON	
	1 onion	
	1 bay leaf	
	4 cloves	
1 litre/1¾ pints	**water**	1 quart
3 × 15ml spoons/ 3 tablespoons	**white wine vinegar**	3 tablespoons
1 × 5ml spoon/ 1 teaspoon	**salt**	1 teaspoon
	4 peppercorns	

Divide the cod fillet into four portions. Wash the fish under the cold tap and pat dry with absorbent paper. To make the court bouillon, peel the onion and make several deep cuts in it. Insert the bay leaf and cloves into the cuts. Bring the water, vinegar and salt to the boil in a large pan, then add the onion and peppercorns. Add the fish to the pan and poach gently for 15 minutes, until done. Meanwhile squeeze the juice from one grapefruit half. Divide the other half into segments, remove pith and skin, chop coarsely and set aside. Remove the fish from the court bouillon and keep warm. Reserve 300 ml/½ pint/1¼ US cups of the liquid.

Melt the butter in a pan. Fry the onion for 5 minutes, until golden. Scatter in the flour and simmer for 3 minutes, stirring. Add the reserved court bouillon and bring to the boil, still stirring. Simmer for 8 minutes. Stir in the cream and grapefruit juice. Put the sauce through a strainer. Season to taste with salt, pepper and a pinch of ground ginger. Arrange the fish on a warmed serving dish, pour the sauce over, and garnish with the eggs and grapefruit pieces. Serve at once.

Oriental Fish with Grapefruit

Kyoto Fish Fillets

Metric/imperial		American
1kg/2 lb	fillets of firm white fish	2 lb
100ml/4 fl oz	sake	½ cup
100ml/4 fl oz	oil	½ cup
3 × 15ml spoons/ 3 tablespoons	sweet rice wine or sweet sherry	3 tablespoons
	6 egg yolks, beaten	
	salt, sugar	

Rinse the fish under cold water, pat dry with absorbent paper, and cut into cubes. Place the cubes in a bowl, pour the sake over them, cover the bowl and allow to stand for 30 minutes. Take out the fish, drain and pat dry. Heat the oil in a large frying pan. Add the fish and fry on all sides for 10 minutes, until just cooked.

Beat the sweet rice wine or sherry into the egg yolks, and season generously with salt and sugar. Pour this mixture over the fish, and cook gently for 3 minutes to allow the egg mixture to thicken. Transfer to a warmed dish and serve at once.

Kyoto Fish Fillets

Steamed Bream

Metric/imperial		American
	1 whole bream or other firm-fleshed sea fish, cleaned	
1 × 5ml spoon/ 1 teaspoon	salt	1 teaspoon
2 × 5ml spoons/ 2 teaspoons	oil	2 teaspoons
	1 leek	
	1 small piece root ginger, finely chopped	
1½ × 15ml spoons/ 1½ tablespoons	sake, Chinese rice wine or dry sherry	1½ tablespoons
1 × 15ml spoon/ 1 tablespoon	soy sauce	1 tablespoon
1 × 2.5ml spoon/ ½ teaspoon	sugar	½ teaspoon
	8 spring onion (scallion) tassels (page 76)	

Do not remove the head and tail when cleaning the fish. Wash the cleaned fish under the cold tap and pat dry with absorbent paper. Make a few, shallow, diagonal cuts on either side of the fish. Rub in the salt and then the oil. Place the fish on its side in a flameproof serving dish just large enough for it. Cut the leek into 5 cm/2 inch strips. Cover the fish with the leek and the chopped ginger. Mix the sake, rice wine or sherry with the soy sauce and sugar, and stir until the sugar has dissolved. Pour this sauce over the fish and place the dish in a large steamer. Steam for 30–40 minutes. Remove the dish from the steamer, arrange the spring onion (scallion) tassels around the fish, and serve at once.

Singapore Fish with Curry Sauce

Metric/imperial		American
	4 × 225g/8 oz halibut steaks	
	juice of 1½ lemons	
100ml/4 fl oz	fish or vegetable stock	½ cup
100ml/4 fl oz	white wine	½ cup
	1 bay leaf	
	salt, pepper	
75g/3 oz	butter	6 tablespoons
30g/1¼ oz	curry powder	⅓ cup
30g/1¼ oz	flour	⅓ cup
150ml/¼ pint	water	⅔ cup
40g/1½ oz	apple purée (sauce)	3 tablespoons
1 × 5ml spoon/ 1 teaspoon	sugar	1 teaspoon
225g/8 oz	button mushrooms	½ lb
	1 banana	

Pat the halibut steaks dry with absorbent paper and sprinkle them with the juice of 1 lemon. Bring the stock and wine to the boil in a large saucepan. Add the bay leaf and salt, and carefully put the fish into the pan. Poach for 10 minutes, until just cooked. Remove the fish from the pan, drain, and arrange on a warmed serving dish. Keep hot. Strain and reserve the fish stock in the pan.

To make the curry sauce, melt 40 g/1½ oz/3 US tablespoons of the butter in a pan, add the curry powder and flour, and cook gently for 3 minutes. Pour the reserved fish stock and the water into the pan, stirring. Bring to the boil and simmer for 5 minutes, then stir in the apple purée (sauce) and season with the remaining lemon juice, salt, pepper and the sugar. Re-heat gently without boiling.

Melt 25 g/1 oz/2 US tablespoons of the butter in a frying pan, and fry the mushrooms for 5 minutes. Season with salt and pepper, remove and keep hot. Peel the banana, cut it in half widthways, then cut each piece in half lengthways. Melt the remaining butter in another frying pan and fry the banana pieces for 2 minutes each side, until golden. To serve, arrange the mushrooms on top of the halibut steaks, garnish with the banana pieces, and pour the sauce around the fish.

Malaysian Fish Curry

Metric/imperial		American
850g/1¾ lb	fillets of firm white fish	1¾ lb
2 × 15ml spoons/ 2 tablespoons	lemon juice	2 tablespoons
	salt, ground ginger	
25g/1 oz	curry powder	¼ cup
	flour for coating	
50ml/2 fl oz	groundnut (peanut) oil	¼ cup
	butter for frying	
	3 onions, sliced	
50ml/2 fl oz	milk	¼ cup
50g/2 oz	peanuts, halved	⅓ cup
150ml/¼ pint	double (heavy) cream	⅔ cup

Wash the fish under the cold tap and pat dry with absorbent paper. Cut into 4 cm/1½ inch cubes and place on a dish. Trickle the lemon juice over the fish, cover and allow to stand for 10 minutes.

Sprinkle salt and half the curry powder over the fish and coat with flour. Heat the oil in a large pan and fry the fish cubes on all sides for 3 minutes, until light brown. Transfer to a serving dish and keep warm. Melt the butter in another pan. Dip the onion rings in milk, then in flour, and fry in the hot fat for 5 minutes, until golden brown. Remove, drain and place over the fish cubes. Add the peanuts to the oil in which the fish was cooked with a pinch each of salt and ground ginger, the cream and remaining curry powder. Simmer gently for 2 minutes over a low heat. Pour over the fish and serve.

South Seas Fish

SERVES 5

Metric/imperial		American
	5 × 225g/8 oz cod steaks	
150ml/¼ pint	lemon juice	⅔ cup
	salt, pepper, ground mace, powdered saffron	
40g/1½ oz	butter	3 tablespoons
	2 onions, chopped	
600ml/1 pint	water	2½ cups
1 × 5ml spoon/ 1 teaspoon	ginger syrup (from preserved stem ginger)	1 teaspoon
	grated rind of 2 lemons	
30g/1¼ oz	flour	⅓ cup
	4 eggs, beaten	
1 × 5ml spoon/ 1 teaspoon	chopped parsley	1 teaspoon

Rinse the fish under cold water and pat dry with absorbent paper. Sprinkle with 1½ × 15ml spoons/1½ tablespoons lemon juice and allow to stand for 10 minutes. Season the fish with salt and pepper. Melt the butter in a large pan and fry the onions until soft, then add the fish steaks and brown on all sides for 5 minutes. Add the water, ginger syrup, lemon rind, remaining lemon juice and a pinch of mace, and bring to the boil. Simmer over low heat for 10 minutes.

Meanwhile stir the flour into the eggs, and season with saffron. Add a little of the liquid from the fish, and season with more salt if necessary. Stir in the parsley. Pour the mixture over the fish. Stirring carefully, bring the contents of the pan to just below boiling point. Take the pan off the heat, arrange the fish in a serving dish, pour on the sauce, and serve at once.

South Seas Fish

Oriental Fish Kebabs

Metric/imperial		American
1kg/2 lb	fillets of red mullet	2 lb
	4 small onions, halved	
	8 small tomatoes, halved	
50ml/2 fl oz	olive oil	¼ cup
2 × 15ml spoons/ 2 tablespoons	sherry	2 tablespoons
1 × 5ml spoon/ 1 teaspoon	sugar	1 teaspoon
	salt, pepper	
	MARINADE	
	1 clove garlic	
	salt	
	juice of 2 lemons	
	SAUCE	
200g/7 oz	yogurt	1 cup
150ml/¼ pint	soured cream	½ cup
1 × 5ml spoon/ 1 teaspoon	chopped parsley	1 teaspoon
1 × 5ml spoon/ 1 teaspoon	chopped chives	1 teaspoon
	salt	

These fish kebabs taste best grilled over charcoal, but an ordinary gas or electric grill (broiler) will still produce good results. Wash the mullet fillets under the cold tap and pat dry with absorbent paper. Cut into slices 1 cm/½ inch thick, across the grain of the flesh. To make the marinade, crush the garlic with salt and mix in a bowl with the lemon juice. Add the fish slices and marinate for 15 minutes, turning frequently.

Meanwhile bring a pan of water to the boil and briefly blanch the onion halves. Drain the fish slices and roll them up. Place alternate rolls of fish, tomato and onion on skewers. Mix the oil, sherry, sugar, and salt and pepper to taste with 2 × 15ml spoons/2 tablespoons of the marinade. Brush the kebabs with this mixture. Put them on a rack under the grill (broiler), with the grill (broiler) pan below to catch the drips. Grill (broil) for 10 minutes, turning frequently, and brushing with the oil, sherry and marinade mixture.

While the kebabs are cooking, prepare the sauce. Beat the yogurt and cream together in a bowl until foamy. Add the parsley and chives and season with salt. Serve the kebabs and sauce separately.

Fish in Soy Sauce

Metric/imperial		American
850g/1¾ lb	whole haddock, cod or mullet, cleaned	1¾ lb
	juice of 1 lemon	
225g/8 oz	pork fillet, thinly sliced	½ lb
	flour for coating	
	1 leek	
80ml/3 fl oz	oil	⅓ cup
	1 piece preserved stem ginger, sliced	
100g/4 oz	bamboo shoots, sliced	¾ cup
150g/5 oz	button mushrooms	2 cups
	FISH MARINADE	
1 × 15ml spoon/ 1 tablespoon	soy sauce	1 tablespoon
1 × 15ml spoon/ 1 tablespoon	Chinese rice wine or dry sherry	1 tablespoon
	salt, pepper, ground ginger	
	MEAT MARINADE	
1 × 15ml spoon/ 1 tablespoon	soy sauce	1 tablespoon
1 × 15ml spoon/ 1 tablespoon	Chinese rice wine or dry sherry	1 tablespoon
1 × 5ml spoon/ 1 teaspoon	flour	1 teaspoon
	SAUCE	
2 × 15ml spoons/ 2 tablespoons	Chinese rice wine or dry sherry	2 tablespoons
2 × 15ml spoons/ 2 tablespoons	soy sauce	2 tablespoons
	sugar, salt	
150ml/¼ pint	fish or vegetable stock	⅔ cup

Cut the head off the fish. Wash the fish under the cold tap and pat dry with absorbent paper. Trickle the lemon juice over it and leave to stand. Mix the ingredients for the fish marinade in a cup. Slash the fish several times across the backbone, put in a dish, pour over the marinade and leave to stand for 30 minutes. Meanwhile coat the pork slices in flour. Mix the ingredients for the meat marinade in a bowl, add the pork and turn from time to time. To make the sauce, mix the rice wine or sherry, soy sauce and a pinch each of sugar and salt in a bowl. Add the stock and keep aside, then cut the leek into strips.

Remove the fish and pork from their marinades and drain. Heat the oil in a pan large enough to take the fish. Add the ginger and leek and fry, stirring, for 5 minutes. Remove from the pan and keep warm. Put the fish in the pan and brown on both sides (2 minutes each side). Add the bamboo shoots, pork and mushrooms, and return the leek and ginger to the pan. Pour the sauce over the fish and vegetables. Cover the pan and bring the contents to boiling point, then reduce the heat and simmer for 15 minutes, until the fish is done. Transfer to a warmed dish and serve.

Fish in Soy Sauce

Crab Omelet with Sherry

Metric/imperial		American
75g/3 oz	canned crabmeat	3 oz
	5 eggs	
	salt, pepper	
2 × 5ml spoons/ 2 teaspoons	dry sherry	2 teaspoons
3 × 15ml spoons/ 3 tablespoons	oil	3 tablespoons
	2 spring onions (scallions), finely chopped	
50g/2 oz	fresh mushrooms, sliced	¾ cup
1 × 15ml spoon/ 1 tablespoon	chopped chives or parsley	1 tablespoon

Drain the crabmeat, reserving the liquid, and remove any hard pieces. Set aside 2 pieces of crabmeat suitable for decoration. Beat the eggs in a bowl, stirring in 1 × 2.5 ml spoon/½ teaspoon salt, pepper to taste and the sherry. Heat half the oil in a wok or frying pan. Add the spring onions (scallions) and mushrooms and fry for 2 minutes, stirring all the time. Add the crabmeat and reserved liquid and cook over a high heat for 2–3 minutes, stirring continuously. Remove the pan from the heat and allow to cool until hand-hot.

Stir the contents of the pan into the egg mixture. Heat the remaining oil in another frying pan, pour in the mixture and fry over a fairly high heat until the underside begins to turn light brown. Turn the omelet over so that the other side sets quickly. Transfer the omelet to a hot serving dish, sprinkle with chives or parsley, and serve garnished with the reserved crabmeat.

Sate Udang

(Prawn [Shrimp] Kebabs)

Metric/imperial		American
450g/1 lb	large prawns (shrimp), peeled (thawed if frozen)	1 lb
1½ × 5ml spoons/ 1½ teaspoons	soy sauce	1½ teaspoons
1 × 2.5ml spoon/ ½ teaspoon	chilli sauce	½ teaspoon
1 × 5ml spoon/ 1 teaspoon	grated root ginger	1 teaspoon
1 × 5ml spoon/ 1 teaspoon	lemon juice	1 teaspoon

Cut the prawns (shrimp) in half lengthways. Remove the black intestinal veins if necessary and then halve them again crossways. Thoroughly mix together the remaining ingredients, add the prawns and leave to marinate for 30 minutes. Thread the quartered prawns on to skewers and grill over a charcoal fire until cooked. Pour the liquid from the marinade over them and serve.

Ga-ti Ming-hsia

Ga-ti Ming-hsia

(Curried Prawns [Shrimp])

Metric/imperial		American
150g/5 oz	canned bamboo shoots	1 cup
15g/½ oz	dried Chinese mushrooms	¾ cup
225g/8 oz	frozen petits pois	½ lb
450g/1 lb	prawns (shrimp), peeled (thawed if frozen)	1 lb
	juice of 1 lemon	
	1 egg white	
25g/1 oz	cornflour (cornstarch)	¼ cup
	oil for deep frying	
	2 onions, chopped	
	ground ginger	
	1 green pepper, de-seeded and chopped	
2 × 5ml spoons/ 2 teaspoons	curry powder	2 teaspoons
1 × 5ml spoon/ 1 teaspoon	sugar	1 teaspoon
2 × 15ml spoons/ 2 tablespoons	soy sauce	2 tablespoons
2 × 15ml spoons/ 2 tablespoons	Chinese rice wine or dry sherry	2 tablespoons

Drain the bamboo shoots, reserving the liquid. Cut the shoots into thin strips. Break the mushrooms into small pieces. Soak them in warm water for 15–30 minutes, until swollen, and then drain. Meanwhile simmer the peas (still frozen) in a little water for 10 minutes, until tender. Drain and keep warm. Pat the prawns (shrimp) dry with absorbent paper. Trickle lemon juice over them. Beat the egg white and cornflour (cornstarch) together, dip the prawns (shrimp) into this batter, and deep fry them in the oil for 2 or 3 minutes. Drain on absorbent paper and keep warm.

Heat 2 × 15ml spoons/2 tablespoons of the frying oil in a pan. Add the onions and bamboo shoots and fry lightly. Add 150 ml/¼ pint/⅔ US cup of the reserved bamboo shoot liquid and a pinch of ground ginger. Bring to the boil and simmer. Add the pepper to the pan when the onions are transparent, and stew briefly with the other vegetables. Season with the curry powder, sugar and soy sauce. Add the drained mushrooms to the pan with the prawns (shrimp) and peas. Warm the rice wine or sherry and pour over the dish before serving.

Sarada Modan

(Japanese Salad)

SERVES 6

Metric/imperial		American
	salt, paprika	
	1 cucumber, grated	
	2 carrots, grated	
	1 large white Japanese radish, grated	
100g/4 oz	fresh mushrooms, sliced	¼ lb
325g/11–12 oz	crayfish tails, halved	¾ lb
1 × 15ml spoon/ 1 tablespoon	chopped parsley	1 tablespoon
1 × 15ml spoon/ 1 tablespoon	chopped borage	1 tablespoon
1 × 15ml spoon/ 1 tablespoon	chopped dill	1 tablespoon
	2 eggs	
	sugar	
50g/2 oz	butter, melted	4 tablespoons
2 × 15ml spoons/ 2 tablespoons	white wine vinegar	2 tablespoons
	1 peach, sliced	
	1 mandarin orange, divided into segments	
	½ orange, sliced	

Sprinkle salt over the grated vegetables and leave for 30 minutes. Pour off the liquid that will have been drawn, then mix the vegetables with the mushrooms. Add the crayfish tails and herbs. Mix and leave to stand for 15 minutes. Meanwhile make the dressing. Whisk together the eggs, a pinch each of salt and sugar, and the butter in a heatproof bowl over a pan of hot water until foamy. Remove the bowl from the heat and gradually stir in the vinegar. Continue stirring until the sauce is cold. Season to taste with paprika. Arrange the grated vegetable mixture in a bowl and pour the sauce over the salad. Garnish with the peach, mandarin orange segments and orange slices.

Chinese Shrimps

Metric/imperial		American
25g/1 oz	raisins	3 tablespoons
100g/4 oz	cooked ham, sliced	$\frac{1}{4}$ lb
50ml/2 fl oz	oil	$\frac{1}{4}$ cup
450g/1 lb	leeks, sliced	1 lb
100g/4 oz	peanuts	$\frac{3}{4}$ cup
250ml/8 fl oz	hot water	1 cup
3 × 15ml spoons/ 3 tablespoons	soy sauce	3 tablespoons
	salt, pepper	
300g/11 oz	boiled shrimps, peeled	scant $\frac{3}{4}$ lb

To plump up the raisins, place them in a metal sieve, pour boiling water over them and drain. Cut the ham slices into thin strips about 4cm/1$\frac{1}{2}$ inches long. Heat the oil in a large pan, add the leeks and fry for 5 minutes, then add the ham, peanuts, raisins and water and simmer for 20 minutes. Add the soy sauce. Season to taste. Finally, add the shrimps and heat through gently.

Chinese Shrimps

Mow-tan-maz

(Chinese Shrimp Cakes)

Metric/imperial		American
	2 small pickled cucumbers	
150g/5 oz	flour	1$\frac{1}{4}$ cups
	2 eggs	
250ml/8 fl oz	water	1 cup
1 × 15ml spoon/ 1 tablespoon	oil	1 tablespoon
225g/8 oz	water chestnuts, chopped	$\frac{1}{2}$ lb
225g/8 oz	boiled shrimps, peeled	$\frac{1}{2}$ lb
	salt, pepper	
	oil for frying	
	sprigs parsley	
	juice of 1 lemon	

Peel the cucumbers and cut into very small dice. Mix the flour, eggs, water and oil to a smooth batter in a bowl. Stir in the water chestnuts, shrimps and cucumber. Season to taste. Heat a little oil in a frying pan. Ladle enough batter into the pan to make a small, thin pancake 10cm/4 inches across. Cook 3 minutes each side, then remove from the pan, drain on absorbent paper and keep warm. Continue until all the batter is used up, adding more frying oil to the pan when necessary. Stack the pancakes on top of each other, in a warm oven, to keep warm. Serve garnished with sprigs of parsley and the lemon juice, served separately.

Mow-tan-maz

Sambal Goreng Udang

(Shrimp Sambal)

Metric/imperial		American
	1 small onion, chopped	
	1 clove garlic, crushed	
1 × 5ml spoon/ 1 teaspoon	ground ginger	1 teaspoon
1 × 5ml spoon/ 1 teaspoon	brown sugar	1 teaspoon
1 × 2.5ml spoon/ ½ teaspoon	belacan (prawn paste)	½ teaspoon
1½ × 5ml spoons/ 1½ teaspoons	chilli sauce	1½ teaspoons
2 × 15ml spoons/ 2 tablespoons	oil	2 tablespoons
	10 peteh beans (see Note)	
1 × 15ml spoon/ 1 tablespoon	tamarind pulp, chopped	1 tablespoon
225g/8 oz	boiled shrimps, peeled	½ lb
	1 bay leaf	
150ml/¼ pint	coconut milk	⅔ cup

Pound and mash together the onion, garlic, ginger, sugar, belacan (prawn paste), and chilli sauce. Heat the oil in a heavy-based pan and fry the mashed ingredients. Add the beans and tamarind, stir, and continue to fry for 1 minute. Stir in the shrimps and fry briefly. Add the bay leaf and coconut milk and simmer for a few minutes. Serve as a side dish.

Note Peteh beans are an almond-shaped variety sold in three forms: fresh, dried, or as a kind of light pickle. The fresh beans are still in their large green pods. The dried beans have a dark brown skin that can be removed after soaking for 30 minutes in warm water. If the pickled beans are bought, their skin will generally have been removed, and the beans are a yellowish-green colour; they only need rinsing before use. As peteh beans can be difficult to obtain, they may be omitted from the recipe.

Tempura

Metric/imperial		American
250g/9 oz	bamboo shoots	1¾ cups
	2 red peppers, de-seeded	
	2 green peppers, de-seeded	
	4 onions, sliced	
400 g/14 oz	prawns (shrimps), peeled (thawed if frozen)	¾–1 lb
	2 pieces preserved stem ginger, sliced	
150g/5 oz	flour	1¼ cups
50g/2 oz	rice flour	6 tablespoons
	8 egg whites	
300ml/½ pint	water	1¼ cups
100ml/4 fl oz	Chinese rice wine or dry sherry	½ cup
	oil for deep frying	

Cut the bamboo shoots into rounds 1 cm/½ inch thick, and cut the peppers into strips. Arrange the bamboo shoots, peppers, onions, prawns (shrimp) and ginger in separate small bowls. Put the flour and rice flour into a bowl. Whisk the egg whites with the water and rice wine or sherry. Stir gradually into the flour until you have a fairly liquid batter. Heat the oil in a fondue dish on the stove until it reaches a temperature of 180°C/350°F, then put the fondue dish over its own burner.

Using a fondue fork, each guest dips his own ingredients in the batter and then deep fries them in the hot oil. Serve individual bowls of boiled rice, with a raw egg yolk broken over the top of each bowl, with this recipe. Serve soy sauce and grated white Japanese radish or horseradish in separate bowls as additional seasoning.

Shrimps Chinese-style

Metric/imperial		American
1½ × 15ml spoons/ 1½ tablespoons	Chinese rice wine or dry sherry	1½ tablespoons
1½ × 15ml spoons/ 1½ tablespoons	soy sauce	1½ tablespoons
1 × 15ml spoon/ 1 tablespoon	cornflour (cornstarch)	1 tablespoon
	salt, ground ginger, garlic salt	
300g/11 oz	boiled shrimps, peeled	scant ¾ lb
20g/¾ oz	butter	4 teaspoons
450g/1 lb	frozen peas	1 lb
3 × 15ml spoons/ 3 tablespoons	water	3 tablespoons
3 × 15ml spoons/ 3 tablespoons	oil	3 tablespoons
	1 leek, sliced	

Mix the rice wine or sherry, soy sauce, cornflour (cornstarch) and a pinch each of ground ginger and garlic salt in a cup. Place the shrimps in a dish, pour over the marinade, cover and leave to stand for 10 minutes. Meanwhile melt the butter in a pan. Add the peas (still frozen) and water, and salt lightly. Simmer, covered, for 6 minutes.

Heat the oil in a pan, add the leek and fry over a high heat for 1 minute. Add the shrimps and marinade and fry for 2 minutes, stirring, then add the peas and fry for 3 minutes longer, stirring carefully. Serve in a warmed dish.

Stir-fried Shrimps

Metric/imperial		American
	1 onion, quartered	
100g/4 oz	fresh bean sprouts	1 cup
	1 large piece canned bamboo shoot	
2 × 15ml spoons/ 2 tablespoons	oil	2 tablespoons
1 × 2.5ml spoon/ ½ teaspoon	salt	½ teaspoon
	1 small piece root ginger, chopped	
350g/12 oz	boiled shrimps, peeled	¾ lb
	1 stick celery, chopped	
2 × 15ml spoons/ 2 tablespoons	sake, Chinese rice wine or dry sherry	2 tablespoons
150ml/¼ pint	chicken stock (page 6)	⅔ cup
2 × 15ml spoons/ 2 tablespoons	cornflour (cornstarch)	2 tablespoons

Cut the onion quarters lengthways into strips. Put the bean sprouts in a pan and pour on boiling water. Rinse under the cold tap until completely cooled, then drain thoroughly. Cut the bamboo shoot lengthways into pieces 2.5 cm/1 inch thick, then cut into strips.

Heat the oil in a wok or frying pan. Add the salt and stir for 20 seconds over a high heat. Add the ginger and the onion and continue stirring for 1–1½ minutes. Add the bamboo shoot and bean sprouts and fry for a further 30–40 seconds, turning the ingredients over thoroughly in the hot oil. Add the shrimps and celery and turn a few times in the oil. Pour in the sake, rice wine or sherry round the edge of the pan and stir in. Add the stock.

To thicken the sauce, mix the cornflour (cornstarch) to a smooth paste with a little cold water in a cup. Blend a little of the hot liquid into the mixture, then return to the pan. Bring slowly to the boil and simmer gently for 2–3 minutes to allow the flour to cook through. Serve immediately.

POULTRY

Bebek-bumbu Bali

(Balinese Duck Curry)

Metric/imperial		American
2kg/4½ lb	duck	4½ lb
2 × 5ml spoons/ 2 teaspoons	salt	2 teaspoons
	2 onions, chopped	
	3 cloves garlic, crushed	
	3 chilli peppers, chopped	
1 × 5ml spoon/ 1 teaspoon	turmeric	1 teaspoon
2 × 5ml spoons/ 2 teaspoons	ground galingale (optional)	2 teaspoons
	belacan (prawn paste)	
3 × 15ml spoons/ 3 tablespoons	oil	3 tablespoons
3 × 15ml spoons/ 3 tablespoons	soy sauce	3 tablespoons
	2 pieces lemon grass (optional)	
	1 bay leaf	
500ml/17 fl oz	boiling water	2 cups

Clean the duck and cut it into 4 pieces. Pound and mix together the salt, onions, garlic, chilli peppers, turmeric, galingale and a little belacan (prawn paste). Heat the oil in a large, heavy pan and fry the spices in it for 3 minutes. Add the duck pieces and soy sauce and continue frying until the duck pieces are brown. Add the lemon grass, bay leaf and water. Cover the pan, bring to the boil, and simmer for 40 minutes, or until the duck is tender. Stir from time to time to prevent sticking. If necessary add more hot water. When the duck is cooked, boil away as much of the liquid as possible. Transfer to a warmed dish and serve with boiled, long-grain rice.

Gano

(Chicken and Pork with Shrimp Omelet)

Metric/imperial		American
1.5kg/3 lb	boiling chicken	3 lb
350g/12 oz	knuckle of pork	¾ lb
	salt, pepper	
200g/7 oz	boiled shrimps, peeled and chopped	scant ½ lb
	2 cloves garlic, crushed	
2 × 15ml spoons/ 2 tablespoons	flour	2 tablespoons
	4 eggs	
1 × 5ml spoon/ 1 teaspoon	water	1 teaspoon
	oil for frying	
25g/1 oz	lard	2 tablespoons
2 × 15ml spoons/ 2 tablespoons	soy sauce	2 tablespoons
	3 white cabbage leaves, shredded	
	1 celery leaf	

Put the chicken and pork in a large saucepan. Season with salt and pour in enough cold water to cover. Bring to the boil, skim off the fat which rises to the surface and simmer, covered, for 2 hours, or until tender.

Pound the shrimps with half the garlic, and the salt, pepper and flour. Separately, beat the eggs with the water and season with salt. Melt a little oil in a frying pan and make 2 omelets, using half the egg mixture for each. Only allow the undersides of the omelets to set. Put half the shrimp mixture into each omelet and roll them up. Finish cooking them in a steamer, over a pan of boiling water, until set. Leave to cool for 30 minutes and cut them across into 1cm/½ inch slices.

Remove the chicken and pork from the stock. Strain the stock. Bone the chicken and pork and cut the flesh into pieces. Melt the lard in a heavy saucepan and fry the remaining garlic. Pour in the stock and bring to the boil. Simmer for 10 minutes. Add the chicken, pork, omelets, soy sauce, cabbage and celery leaf, and heat through. Serve at once in warmed bowls.

Chinese Chicken with Shrimps and Bamboo Shoots

Metric/imperial		American
1kg/2 lb	chicken breasts or thighs, boned	2 lb
	salt, pepper	
150g/5 oz	bamboo shoots	1 cup
100ml/4 fl oz	oil	½ cup
150g/5 oz	prawns or shrimps, peeled	5 oz
100g/4 oz	fresh mushrooms, sliced	¼ lb
900ml/1½ pints	chicken stock (page 6)	1 quart
1½ × 15ml spoons/ 1½ tablespoons	cornflour (cornstarch)	1½ tablespoons
3 × 15ml spoons/ 3 tablespoons	soy sauce	3 tablespoons
1 × 5ml spoon/ 1 teaspoon	sugar	1 teaspoon
1 × 5ml spoon/ 1 teaspoon	sambal baatjak (see **Note**)	1 teaspoon
1 × 15ml spoon/ 1 tablespoon	spare rib sauce (see **Note**)	1 tablespoon
	5 large prawns (shrimp), peeled	

Cut the chicken pieces into strips and season with salt. Cut the bamboo shoots into strips. Heat the oil in a frying pan, add the chicken and fry until golden brown (5 minutes). Add the bamboo shoots and fry for 15 minutes. Add the shrimps or prawns and mushrooms, and continue frying gently for 10 minutes, stirring from time to time.

Meanwhile make the sauce. Bring the stock to the boil in a pan. Mix the cornflour (cornstarch) to a smooth paste with a little cold water in a cup. Blend a little of the hot stock into the mixture, then return to the pan. Bring slowly to the boil, stirring constantly. Simmer for 2–3 minutes to allow the flour to cook through. Season with the soy sauce, sugar, salt and pepper. Add the sauce to the chicken and shrimp mixture. Cover the pan and leave to simmer, very gently, for 5 minutes. Adjust seasoning to taste with sambal baatjak and spare rib sauce.

Serve this dish with boiled, long-grain rice. Arrange the rice in a serving dish, pour the chicken mixture into the centre and garnish with the large prawns (shrimp).
Note Sambal baatjak is an Indonesian relish and can be bought ready-prepared from oriental food shops. Spare rib sauce can also be bought ready-prepared.

Chinese Chicken with Shrimps and Bamboo Shoots

Peking Duck

Metric/imperial		American
1.5kg/3 lb	duck (see **Notes**)	3 lb
80ml/3 fl oz	water	6 tablespoons
4–5 × 15ml spoons/ 4–5 tablespoons	honey	4–5 tablespoons

Peking duck is one of the most famous of all Chinese dishes; its special feature is the crisp, tasty skin which is served separately.

Ask the poulterer for a good duck, as fresh as possible. The feathers should be on, the skin as intact as possible, and the bird should still have its neck, with skin. Pluck the bird. Plunge in boiling water long enough to blanch the skin. Dry thoroughly, inside and out. Skewer or stitch up the vent firmly. Tie a piece of string under the wings and round the neck, and hang in a cool, well-ventilated place, by an open window for example, for a couple of hours until the skin is completely dry.

Bring the water to the boil and stir in the honey until fully dissolved. Leave to cool until tepid, then spread the honey mixture over the duck in several applications, pausing after each one, until the skin is impregnated with the honey. Hang the bird up again until the skin has completely dried.

Place the duck on a rack in a roasting pan. Roast until the duck is brown, 1–1½ hours at 190°C/375°F/Gas 5. Check that the skin browns evenly; any patches that look as though they are turning too dark should be covered with aluminium foil. The duck is then removed from the oven, and the skin is removed and carved into long, thin strips.

The correct way to eat Peking duck is with pancakes, hoisin or plum sauce and spring onion tassels (see page 76). A slice of skin and a spring onion tassel are placed on a sauce-covered pancake, which is then rolled up and eaten with the fingers.

Notes Before being sewn up and hung to dry, the duck can be smeared inside with a paste made up of 1 × 2.5ml spoon/½ teaspoon each salt, five-spice powder and hoisin sauce, 1 × 5ml spoon/1 teaspoon soy sauce, and 1 × 15ml spoon/1 tablespoon Chinese rice wine or dry sherry.

Sometimes a slit is made in the skin where the neck joins the body. A straw is inserted and air is blown under the skin so that it comes away from the flesh and balloons out. The neck is then tied with string just below the slit. This treatment makes the skin even crisper and tastier.

Traditional Peking duck is a dish which, even in China, is almost exclusively prepared by experts in restaurants where it is a speciality. Because of the specially-bred ducks, the elaborate and time-consuming preparation and special oven in which the duck should be roasted, the same sort of result should not be expected when prepared in the home.

Chinese Duck

Metric/imperial		American
600ml/1 pint + 75ml/2½ fl oz	dry sherry	2½ cups + ⅓ cup
2 × 15ml spoons/ 2 tablespoons	honey	2 tablespoons
2 × 15ml spoons/ 2 tablespoons	soy sauce	2 tablespoons
	2 small pieces preserved stem ginger, chopped	
1 × 5ml spoon/ 1 teaspoon	mustard powder	1 teaspoon
1 × 5ml spoon/ 1 teaspoon	sesame seeds	1 teaspoon
1.5kg/3 lb	oven-ready duck	3 lb
	salt	
40g/1½ oz	margarine	3 tablespoons
	rind of ½ orange	
	juice of 6 oranges	
25g/1 oz	sugar	2 tablespoons
1½ × 15ml spoons/ 1½ tablespoons	cornflour (cornstarch)	1½ tablespoons
200g/7 oz	canned mandarin oranges, drained	scant ½ lb
	1 banana, sliced	
	1 orange, sliced	
	2 cherries	
	sprigs parsley	

Mix the 600ml/1 pint/2½ US cups sherry with the honey and soy sauce. Stir in half the ginger, the mustard powder and sesame seeds. Marinate the duck in this mixture for 3 hours, covered, turning the duck from time to time. Take the duck out of the marinade, drain well and season with salt inside. Melt the margarine in a roasting pan and brown the duck on all sides. Place the pan in the oven and roast for 1 hour 10 minutes at 200°C/400°F/Gas 6, basting with the marinade every so often.

Cut the orange rind into very thin strips. Chop the remaining ginger very finely. Mix together the orange rind and juice, ginger, sugar and 2½ × 15ml spoons/ 2½ tablespoons sherry in a pan. Heat gently. Mix the cornflour (cornstarch) to a smooth paste in a cup with the remaining sherry. Blend a little of the hot liquid into the mixture, then return to the pan. Bring slowly to the boil, stirring constantly. Simmer for 2–3 minutes to allow the flour to cook through. Then add half of the mandarin oranges and banana slices to the sauce and heat through gently.

Place the cooked duck on a warmed serving dish. Arrange the remaining mandarin oranges, and the slices of orange topped with the remaining banana slices, around the duck. Garnish with the cherries and sprigs of parsley. Serve the sauce separately.

Overleaf: Chinese Duck

Mo-ku-chi-pien

(Stir-fried Chicken with Mushrooms)

Metric/imperial		American
850g/1¾ lb	chicken breasts or thighs, boned	1¾ lb
80ml/3 fl oz	Chinese rice wine or dry sherry	6 tablespoons
1½ × 15ml spoons/ 1½ tablespoons	flour	1½ tablespoons
	salt, pepper, ground ginger	
80ml/3 fl oz	oil	6 tablespoons
150g/5 oz	peas	1 cup
150g/5 oz	fresh button mushrooms	2 cups
1 × 15ml spoon/ 1 tablespoon	soy sauce	1 tablespoon
	meat extract	
1 × 5ml spoon/ 1 teaspoon	cornflour (cornstarch)	1 teaspoon

Cut the chicken meat into pieces and place in a bowl. Mix together 60ml/4 tablespoons of the rice wine or sherry and the flour in a cup. Season with salt and pepper. Pour this marinade over the chicken pieces, cover, and leave to stand for 10 minutes.

Heat 2 × 15ml spoons/2 tablespoons of the oil in a frying pan. Fry the peas and mushrooms for 2 minutes, stirring. Season with salt. Remove the vegetables from the pan and keep warm. Add the remaining oil to the pan and heat. Stir the chicken pieces and marinade into the pan and fry for 5 minutes, stirring all the time. Return the vegetables to the pan and mix with the chicken. Season to taste with salt, soy sauce, a small pinch of ground ginger and a small amount of meat extract dissolved in a little hot water.

Mix the cornflour (cornstarch) to a smooth paste with the remaining rice wine or sherry and add to the pan, stirring. Let the contents of the pan come to the boil, adjust the seasoning if necessary, and serve.

Mo-ku-chi-pien

Singgang Ayam

(Stewed and Grilled Chicken)

Metric/imperial		American
1kg/2 lb	**chicken** (see **Note**)	2 lb
	1 small onion, chopped	
	2 cloves garlic, crushed	
1 × 2.5ml spoon/ ½ teaspoon	**chilli paste**	½ teaspoon
	1 small piece root ginger, chopped	
1 × 2.5ml spoon/ ½ teaspoon	**pepper**	½ teaspoon
1 × 2.5ml spoon/ ½ teaspoon	**turmeric**	½ teaspoon
1 × 2.5ml spoon/ ½ teaspoon	**ground galingale** (optional)	½ teaspoon
1 × 5ml spoon/ 1 teaspoon	**salt**	1 teaspoon
	1 piece lemon grass (optional)	
500ml/17 fl oz	**coconut milk**	2 cups

Cut the chicken open down the breast. Open the two halves outwards and press flat by breaking the breast bones where they are attached to the back. Push a wooden skewer through the legs and the back so that the bird is held flat, and skewer the wings into position in the same way. Pound and mix together all the ingredients except the lemon grass and coconut milk. Rub the mixture into the chicken meat and leave for 1½ hours to absorb the flavours.

Bring the coconut milk to the boil in a large saucepan. Add the lemon grass and chicken. Simmer over moderate heat, with the pan uncovered, until the chicken is almost done (45 minutes–1 hour). Remove the chicken from the pan and grill it over charcoal until golden brown. Trickle some of the cooking liquid over it from time to time. Remove the skewers and serve.

Note The chicken for this recipe should be young, fresh and tender.

Indonesian Chicken Kebabs

Metric/imperial		American
	4 × 350g/12 oz chicken breasts, skinned and boned	
100g/4 oz	chopped walnuts	1 cup
300ml/½ pint	lime or lemon juice	1¼ cups
250ml/8 fl oz	hot chicken stock (page 6)	1 cup
	salt, pepper	
	1 clove garlic	
	1 onion, chopped	
2 × 15ml spoons/ 2 tablespoons	oil	2 tablespoons
150ml/¼ pint	double (heavy) cream	⅔ cup
	sprigs parsley	

Cut the chicken into pieces suitable for threading on to skewers. Mix the walnuts, lime or lemon juice, stock, salt and pepper in a bowl. Crush the garlic with salt and add to the marinade with the onion. Put one third of the marinade aside and add the chicken pieces to the remainder. Cover and allow to stand for 3 hours.

Drain the chicken and pat dry on absorbent paper. Thread the chicken pieces on to skewers and brush them with the oil. Cover the rack of the grill (broiler) with aluminium foil, place the skewers on it and grill (broil) for 20 minutes, turning once. Drain the reserved marinade and mix with the cream to make a sauce. Heat gently in a pan without boiling. Serve the kebabs, on a warmed dish and garnish with the sprigs of parsley. Serve the sauce separately.

Indonesian Chicken Kebabs

Oriental Spiced Chicken

Oriental Spiced Chicken

SERVES 6

Metric/imperial		American
	2 × 850g/1¾ lb chickens	
2 × 5ml spoons/ 2 teaspoons	curry powder	2 teaspoons
2 × 5ml spoons/ 2 teaspoons	mild paprika	2 teaspoons
1 × 5ml spoon/ 1 teaspoon	black pepper	1 teaspoon
	salt	
2 × 15ml spoons/ 2 tablespoons	oil	2 tablespoons
50ml/2 fl oz	single (light) cream	¼ cup
2 × 15ml spoons/ 2 tablespoons	lemon juice	2 tablespoons
1 × 5ml spoon/ 1 teaspoon	ground coriander	1 teaspoon
1 × 5ml spoon/ 1 teaspoon	ground cardamom	1 teaspoon
	oil for deep frying	

Cut each chicken into 4 portions. Mix together the curry powder, paprika, pepper and a pinch of salt on a plate. Toss the chicken portions in this mixture and place them in a shallow dish. Stir the oil, cream and lemon juice together in a cup, and pour over the chicken pieces. Sprinkle with the coriander and cardamom. Allow to stand for 30 minutes, turning from time to time. Remove the chicken portions from the marinade and pat dry with absorbent paper.

Heat the oil to a temperature of 180°C/350°F. Deep fry the chicken portions, in 2 batches, for 15 minutes each. Keep the first batch hot while you fry the second. Arrange in a warmed dish and serve.

Chicken in Soy Sauce

Metric/imperial		American
1.5kg/3 lb	chicken, skinned and boned	3 lb
1 × 15ml spoon/ 1 tablespoon	cornflour (cornstarch)	1 tablespoon
2 × 15ml spoons/ 2 tablespoons	Chinese rice wine or dry sherry	2 tablespoons
3 × 15ml spoons/ 3 tablespoons	soy sauce	3 tablespoons
	1 egg white	
	1 leek	
100ml/4 fl oz	oil	½ cup
500g/18 oz	bean sprouts	generous 1 lb
	pepper, ground ginger	

Cut the chicken into thin pieces about 3cm/1¼ inches in size. Mix the cornflour (cornstarch) in a bowl with the rice wine or sherry and 1 × 15ml spoon/1 tablespoon soy sauce. Whisk the egg white lightly with a fork and stir into the marinade. Add the chicken pieces and allow to stand for 30 minutes.

Meanwhile cut the leek in half lengthways and then into thin strips 2cm/¾ inch long. Heat half of the oil in a large, shallow pan. Fry the leek for 3 minutes, stirring. Add the bean sprouts and fry for another 2 minutes. Season with pepper, the remaining soy sauce and a small pinch of ground ginger. Heat the remaining oil in another pan. Remove the chicken pieces from the marinade, drain and fry in the oil for 5 minutes until golden brown on all sides. Transfer to the vegetable pan and fry for another 3 minutes, stirring all the time. Arrange on a warmed dish and serve at once.

Sate Ayam

(Chicken Kebabs)

Metric/imperial		American
1kg/2 lb	chicken, skinned and boned (see Note)	2 lb
1 × 2.5ml spoon/ ½ teaspoon	salt	½ teaspoon
1 × 2.5ml spoon/ ½ teaspoon	belacan (prawn paste)	½ teaspoon
	2 cloves garlic, crushed	
	pinch of pepper	
3 × 15ml spoons/ 3 tablespoons	soy sauce	3 tablespoons
1 × 15ml spoon/ 1 tablespoon	lemon juice	1 tablespoon
1 × 15ml spoon/ 1 tablespoon	oil	1 tablespoon

Cut the chicken meat into cubes suitable for threading on to skewers. In a bowl, mash together the salt, belacan (prawn paste), garlic and a pinch of pepper. Add the soy sauce and lemon juice and stir well. Add the oil and chicken pieces. Stir thoroughly and leave to marinate for 30 minutes.

Remove the chicken pieces from the marinade, drain and thread them on to small kebab skewers. Grill over a charcoal fire if possible, although an ordinary gas or electric grill (broiler) will still produce good results. Baste with the marinade from time to time, and grill the kebabs until they are brown and tender. Serve immediately.

Note The chicken for this recipe should be young, fresh and tender.

Chinese Fried Chicken

Metric/imperial		American
	1 leek	
1kg/2 lb	boiling chicken	2 lb
2 × 15ml spoons/ 2 tablespoons	soy sauce	2 tablespoons
2 × 15ml spoons/ 2 tablespoons	Chinese rice wine or dry sherry	2 tablespoons
	pinch of ground ginger	
40g/1½ oz	flour	6 tablespoons
	1 egg	
	oil for deep frying	

Cut the leek in half lengthways and cut into thin strips. Bring a large pan of lightly salted water to the boil. Add the chicken, leek, soy sauce, half the rice wine or sherry and a pinch of ground ginger. Simmer for 1½ hours until the chicken is tender.

Remove the chicken from the pan and drain. Reserve 4 × 15ml spoons/4 tablespoons of the chicken stock. Remove the bones from the chicken, cut the meat into strips and allow to cool. Trickle the rest of the rice wine or sherry over the meat. While the chicken is cooling, mix the flour and egg to a smooth batter with the reserved chicken stock. Coat the chicken strips with the batter and deep fry in hot oil until golden brown. Drain on absorbent paper and serve at once.

MEAT

Cantonese Pork

Metric/imperial		American
1kg/2 lb	pork fillet in one piece	2 lb
1 × 15ml spoon/ 1 tablespoon	soy sauce	1 tablespoon
2 × 15ml spoons/ 2 tablespoons	chicken stock (page 6)	2 tablespoons
1 × 15ml spoon/ 1 tablespoon	honey	1 tablespoon
1 × 15ml spoon/ 1 tablespoon	sugar	1 tablespoon
1 × 5ml spoon/ 1 teaspoon	dayong (see Note)	1 teaspoon
	salt	
2 × 15ml spoons/ 2 tablespoons	oil	2 tablespoons

Pat the pork dry with absorbent paper. Mix the soy sauce, stock, honey, sugar and dayong in a bowl. Season with salt. Spread this mixture over the pork and rub in well. Put the pork in a bowl, cover, and leave to stand for 1 hour. Remove and drain, reserving the marinade. Rub the oil into the pork, put into an ovenproof dish, and paint with the reserved marinade. Cover and place on the middle shelf of the oven. Bake for 1 hour 20 minutes at 200°C/400°F/Gas 6. Remove from the oven and serve in the dish with bamboo shoot salad (page 77), boiled, long-grain rice and mushrooms.

Note Dayong is obtainable ready-prepared from oriental food shops.

Cantonese Pork

Cau Tju Juk

(Chinese Belly of Pork)

Metric/imperial		American
1kg/2 lb	lean belly of pork, with the rind on, in one piece	2 lb
	garlic salt, ground star anise, ground ginger	
1 × 15ml spoon/ 1 tablespoon	soy sauce	1 tablespoon
2 × 15ml spoons/ 2 tablespoons	groundnut (peanut) oil	2 tablespoons
300ml/½ pint	hot water	1¼ cups
	SAUCE	
200g/7 oz	red peppers, de-seeded and chopped	scant ½ lb
25g/1 oz	canned apricots, drained	2 tablespoons
	1 clove garlic	
	salt	
	grated rind of ½ lemon	
1 × 15ml spoon/ 1 tablespoon	chilli sauce	1 tablespoon
2 × 15ml spoons/ 2 tablespoons	soy sauce	2 tablespoons
	GARNISH	
	1 red pepper, sliced	
	2 cloves star anise	

Wash and scrub the pork rind and pat dry with absorbent paper. Make cuts across it to form a diamond pattern. Mix together a pinch each of garlic salt, ground star anise and ground ginger in a bowl with the soy sauce and groundnut (peanut) oil. Rub this mixture well into the meat. Lay the meat on a rack in a roasting pan, and place on the middle shelf of the oven. Pour the water into the roasting pan and roast for 1 hour 40 minutes at 200°C/400°F/Gas 6. Baste the meat from time to time with the liquid from the pan. While the meat is roasting, make the sauce.

Bring a pan of lightly salted water to the boil. Add the peppers and simmer for 20 minutes. Drain and cool slightly. Purée the peppers with the apricots in a liquidizer (blender), or strain through a sieve. Crush the garlic clove with salt and mix into the pepper and apricot purée. Add the lemon rind, chilli sauce and soy sauce, and mix.

Take the meat out of the oven and arrange on a warmed dish. Garnish with the red pepper and cloves of star anise. Serve the sauce separately with a bowl of boiled, long-grain rice.

Chinese Belly of Pork

Chinese Roast Belly of Pork

Metric/imperial		American
1kg/2 lb	lean belly of pork, with the rind on, in one piece	2 lb
	salt	
1½ × 5ml spoons/ 1½ teaspoons	brown sugar	1½ teaspoons
2 × 15ml spoons/ 2 tablespoons	soy sauce	2 tablespoons
1 × 5ml spoon/ 1 teaspoon	chopped root ginger	1 teaspoon
	hoisin sauce	

Prick holes in the pork rind and rub well with salt. Mix together the sugar, soy sauce, ginger and hoisin sauce. Rub this mixture into the other side of the pork. Place the pork on a flat grill (broiler) pan with the rind uppermost, and grill (broil) for 20 minutes, until the rind is crisp all over. Transfer to the oven and roast for 1 hour at 180°C/350°F/Gas 4. Remove from the oven and allow to cool to room temperature. Cut the meat into small chunks and serve with stir-fried Chinese cabbage (see page 74). Watercress and spring onions (scallions) are also good accompaniments to the dish.

Chinese Roast Belly of Pork with Bean Curd

Metric/imperial		American
	½ recipe Chinese roast belly of pork (see left)	
	1 cake bean curd	
2–3 × 15ml spoons/ 2–3 tablespoons	soy sauce	2–3 tablespoons
100ml/4 fl oz	chicken stock (page 6)	½ cup
1 × 2.5ml spoon/ ½ teaspoon	salt	½ teaspoon
1 × 2.5ml spoon/ ½ teaspoon	sugar	½ teaspoon
1 × 15ml spoon/ 1 tablespoon	cornflour (cornstarch)	1 tablespoon
2 × 15ml spoons/ 2 tablespoons	water	2 tablespoons
1½ × 15ml spoons/ 1½ tablespoons	oil	1½ tablespoons
	sprigs parsley	

Prepare and cook the roast belly of pork as described left, but using half the ingredients and a shorter roasting time (about 45 minutes). Remove from the oven when cooked and allow to cool.

While the pork is cooking, cut the bean curd into chunks 4 × 2 × 2cm/1½ × ¾ × ¾ inch. When the pork has cooled, cut it into similar-sized chunks. Put the soy sauce, stock, salt and sugar in a saucepan. Heat the mixture until the salt and sugar dissolve. Mix the cornflour (cornstarch) to a smooth paste in a cup with the water.

Heat the oil in a wok or frying pan. Add the bean curd and fry, stirring, until just coloured on all sides. Pour on the soy sauce mixture and simmer over low heat for 7 minutes. Add the cornflour (cornstarch) paste and stir over a high heat until the sauce is thick and shiny. Add the pork to the pan and heat through. Sprinkle with parsley and serve with boiled, long-grain rice.

Chinese Pork and Peas

Metric/imperial		American
350g/12 oz	pork fillet	¾ lb
100ml/4 fl oz	oil	½ cup
100g/4 oz	peas	¾ cup
150ml/¼ pint	hot meat stock (page 7)	⅔ cup
	salt, pepper, ground ginger, sugar	
	1 leek	
	1 clove garlic, chopped	
100g/4 oz	mushrooms, sliced	¼ lb
100g/4 oz	bamboo shoots, sliced	¾ cup
	1 piece preserved stem ginger, sliced	
1 × 15ml spoon/ 1 tablespoon	Chinese rice wine or dry sherry	1 tablespoon
1 × 15ml spoon/ 1 tablespoon	cornflour (cornstarch)	1 tablespoon
2 × 15ml spoons/ 2 tablespoons	oyster sauce	2 tablespoons
2 × 5ml spoons/ 2 teaspoons	soy sauce	2 teaspoons
	MARINADE	
2 × 15ml spoons/ 2 tablespoons	soy sauce	2 tablespoons
2 × 5ml spoons/ 2 teaspoons	Chinese rice wine or dry sherry	2 teaspoons
	1 egg white	
1 × 5ml spoon/ 1 teaspoon	cornflour (cornstarch)	1 teaspoon
	salt, pepper	

Slice the pork fillet thinly, cutting diagonally across the grain of the meat. Cut the slices into strips. To make the marinade, beat together the soy sauce, rice wine or sherry, egg white and cornflour (cornstarch) in a bowl. Season to taste. Put the meat into the marinade, cover, and place in the refrigerator for 30 minutes.

Meanwhile, heat 2 × 15ml spoons/2 tablespoons oil in a small saucepan. Add the peas and stock, season with salt and sugar, and simmer for 5 minutes. Pour off and reserve the stock. Keep the peas warm. Cut the leek into strips. Heat 3 × 15ml spoons/3 tablespoons oil in a large pan. Add the leek, garlic, mushrooms, bamboo shoots and stem ginger and fry for 5 minutes, stirring all the time. Remove from the heat and keep warm.

Heat the remaining oil in another pan. Add the meat with its marinade and fry for 3 minutes, stirring frequently. Add to the vegetable pan together with the peas. Stir in the rice wine or sherry, and the reserved stock from the peas. Mix the cornflour (cornstarch) to a smooth paste with the oyster sauce and soy sauce. Stir into the pan. Bring the contents of the pan to the boil. Season to taste with salt, pepper, ground ginger and sugar. Serve at once.

Babi Cin

(Spicy Pork, Potatoes and Onions)

Metric/imperial		American
850g/1¾ lb	fat belly of pork	1¾ lb
	2 cloves garlic, crushed	
	1 small piece root ginger, chopped or 1 × 5ml spoon/ 1 teaspoon ground ginger	
1 × 2.5ml spoon/ ½ teaspoon	ground coriander	½ teaspoon
1 × 15ml spoon/ 1 tablespoon	soya bean paste	1 tablespoon
2 × 15ml spoons/ 2 tablespoons	soy sauce	2 tablespoons
	salt, pepper	
50g/2 oz	lard	¼ cup
250–500ml/ 8–17 fl oz	hot meat stock (page 7)	1–2 cups
300g/11 oz	small new potatoes, peeled	scant ¾ lb
	6 button (pickling) onions, halved	
	2 spring onions (scallions), finely chopped	
	½ stick celery, finely chopped	

Cut the pork into cubes. Pound and mix together the garlic, ginger, coriander and soya bean paste. Stir in the soy sauce and season with salt and pepper. Add the meat and mix thoroughly.

Heat half the lard in a saucepan, add the meat and brown on all sides. Add 250ml/8 fl oz/1 US cup stock, bring to the boil, reduce the heat and simmer gently until all the fat has been drawn out.

Meanwhile heat the remaining lard in another pan. Add the potatoes and fry gently until almost done (test with a fork). Remove and keep warm. Add the button (pickling) onions to the pan in which the potatoes were cooked, and fry for a few minutes. Skim off the fat which will have risen to the top of the meat pan, then add the potatoes and onions to the meat, pouring on more stock if necessary. Add the spring onions (scallions) and celery and simmer for a further 5 minutes before serving.

Babi Cin

Daging Masak Tomat

(Meat in Tomato Sauce)

Metric/imperial		American
450g/1 lb	pork	1 lb
	5 ripe tomatoes, skinned, de-seeded and chopped	
	4 red onions, chopped	
	1 small piece root ginger, chopped or 2 × 5ml spoons/ 2 teaspoons ground ginger	
	2–3 red chilli peppers, chopped or 2 × 5ml spoons/ 2 teaspoons chilli sauce	
	1 piece lemon grass	
1 × 2.5ml spoon/ ½ teaspoon	sugar	½ teaspoon
1 × 5ml spoon/ 1 teaspoon	salt	1 teaspoon
300ml/½ pint	water	1¼ cups
	1 spring onion (scallion), chopped or 2 × 5ml spoons/ 2 teaspoons chopped chives	

Cut the pork, which should be edged with fat, into chunks. Thoroughly mix together all the remaining ingredients, except for the spring onion (scallion) or chives. Put the mixed ingredients into a saucepan and bring to the boil. Reduce the heat and simmer gently for 45 minutes–1 hour, until the meat is cooked and the sauce has thickened, adding a little extra water if necessary. Just before serving, stir in the spring onion (scallion) or chives, allowing another 1–2 minutes for them to heat through. Serve immediately.

Daging Masak Tomat

Sweet-and-sour Pork

Metric/imperial		American
600g/1¼ lb	pork, cubed	1¼ lb
	oil for deep frying	
	MARINADE	
	1 egg white	
40g/1½ oz	cornflour (cornstarch)	6 tablespoons
2 × 15ml spoons/ 2 tablespoons	soy sauce	2 tablespoons
2 × 15ml spoons/ 2 tablespoons	Chinese rice wine or dry sherry	2 tablespoons
	salt, pepper	
	BATTER	
	1 egg	
50g/2 oz	flour	½ cup
150ml/¼ pint	lager (light beer)	⅔ cup
	salt	
	SAUCE	
2 × 15ml spoons/ 2 tablespoons	oil	2 tablespoons
	1 small red pepper, de-seeded and chopped	
	1 small green pepper, de-seeded and chopped	
200g/7 oz	bamboo shoots, chopped	1⅓ cups
	3 canned pineapple rings, drained and chopped	
600ml/1 pint	hot chicken stock (page 6)	2½ cups
3 × 15ml spoons/ 3 tablespoons	soy sauce	3 tablespoons
2 × 15ml spoons/ 2 tablespoons	vinegar	2 tablespoons
3 × 15ml spoons/ 3 tablespoons	tomato ketchup	3 tablespoons
50g/2 oz	sugar	¼ cup
	salt	
20g/¾ oz	cornflour (cornstarch)	3 tablespoons

Make the marinade first: beat the egg white in a bowl with the cornflour (cornstarch). Mix in the soy sauce and rice wine or sherry, and season to taste. Put the pork cubes into the marinade and leave for 15 minutes, turning frequently.

To make the batter, whisk together the egg, flour, lager and salt in a bowl. Remove the pork from the marinade and drain well. Dip into the batter and deep fry for 4 minutes, a few at a time. Remove, drain and keep warm.

To make the sauce, heat the oil in a saucepan, and add the peppers, bamboo shoots and pineapple. Fry, stirring, for 2 minutes. Add the stock, soy sauce, vinegar, tomato ketchup and sugar, and stir. Season with salt and simmer for 5 minutes. Mix the cornflour (cornstarch) to a smooth paste with a little cold water. Blend a little of the hot liquid into the mixture, then return to the pan. Bring slowly to the boil, stirring constantly. Simmer for 2–3 minutes to allow the flour to cook through. Arrange the pork on a warmed serving dish and pour the hot sauce over.

Szechuan Pork

Metric/imperial		American
850g/1¾ lb	boneless lean pork	1¾ lb
100ml/4 fl oz	oil	½ cup
150g/5 oz	fresh mushrooms, sliced	2 cups
200g/7 oz	green peppers, de-seeded and chopped	1⅓ cups
200g/7 oz	tomatoes, sliced	scant ½ lb
	salt, ground ginger	
200g/7 oz	onions, finely chopped	2 cups
	1 clove garlic, crushed	
2 × 15ml spoons/ 2 tablespoons	Chinese rice wine or dry sherry	2 tablespoons
300ml/½ pint	hot meat stock (page 7)	1¼ cups
1 × 15ml spoon/ 1 tablespoon	soy sauce	1 tablespoon
20g/¾ oz	cornflour (cornstarch)	3 tablespoons

Cut the pork into thin strips 5cm/2 inches long. Heat half the oil in a frying pan. Add the mushrooms, peppers and tomatoes and fry gently for 5 minutes. Remove from the pan, drain and keep warm. Heat the remaining oil in another pan. Add the meat. Sprinkle with salt and a pinch of ground ginger and fry for 10 minutes, stirring. Add the onions and garlic and fry for another 5 minutes. Pour in the rice wine or sherry and heat through briefly, then add the stock and soy sauce. Finally, add the reserved mushroom, pepper and tomato mixture. Cover the pan and stew gently over medium heat for 25 minutes.

Mix the cornflour (cornstarch) to a smooth paste in a cup with a little cold water. Blend a little of the hot liquid into the mixture, then return to the pan. Bring slowly to the boil, stirring constantly. Simmer for 2–3 minutes to allow the flour to cook through. Transfer the contents of the pan to a warmed dish and serve.

Szechuan Pork

Chinese Liver

Metric/imperial		American
450g/1 lb	pig's liver	1 lb
	flour for coating	
	1 red pepper, de-seeded	
	1 green pepper, de-seeded	
200g/7 oz	savoy cabbage	scant ½ lb
5 × 15ml spoons/ 5 tablespoons	oil	⅓ cup
	salt, pepper	
3 × 15ml spoons/ 3 tablespoons	soy sauce	3 tablespoons
2 × 15ml spoons/ 2 tablespoons	Chinese rice wine or dry sherry	2 tablespoons
200g/7 oz	onions, sliced	scant ½ lb
300ml/½ pint	meat stock (page 7)	1¼ cups
150g/5 oz	bean sprouts	1½ cups
150g/5 oz	canned bamboo shoots, chopped	1 cup

Chinese Liver

Pat the liver dry with absorbent paper and cut it into narrow strips. Toss in the flour. Cut the peppers and cabbage into strips. Heat the oil in a frying pan, add the liver and brown on all sides. Remove from the pan, drain, season to taste and keep warm. Add the soy sauce and rice wine or sherry to the pan. Add the onions and simmer for 5 minutes. Add the stock, peppers, and cabbage and simmer for about 10 minutes, until just tender. Return the liver to the pan. Add the bean sprouts and bamboo shoots. Reheat and serve with boiled, long-grain rice and extra soy sauce sprinkled on top if desired.

Peking Beef

Metric/imperial		American
450g/1 lb	fillet of beef	1 lb
5 × 15ml spoons/ 5 tablespoons	soy sauce	⅓ cup
1 × 15ml spoon/ 1 tablespoon	Chinese rice wine or dry sherry	1 tablespoon
300ml/½ pint	oil	1¼ cups
	flour for coating	
	2 cloves garlic	
	salt, ground ginger, ground aniseed	
	2 leeks, finely sliced	
1 × 15ml spoon/ 1 tablespoon	ginger syrup (from preserved stem ginger)	1 tablespoon
150ml/¼ pint	meat stock (page 7)	⅔ cup
1 × 5ml spoon/ 1 teaspoon	cornflour (cornstarch)	1 teaspoon

Pat the meat dry with absorbent paper. Cut into very thin slices diagonally, across the grain of the meat. Mix 3 × 15ml spoons/3 tablespoons of the soy sauce with the rice wine or sherry in a deep bowl. Add the meat, cover, and leave to marinate for 1 hour.

Heat the oil in a frying pan. Take the meat out of the marinade, drain well and dust with flour. Add to the oil and fry for 3 minutes. Remove the meat, drain and set aside. Crush the garlic cloves with salt. Take 4 × 15ml spoons/ 4 tablespoons of the frying oil and put it in another pan. Heat the oil, add the garlic and leeks, and fry for 5 minutes, stirring. Add the meat. Season with the ginger syrup, a pinch of ground ginger, the remaining soy sauce and a small pinch of ground aniseed. Pour the stock into the pan. Remove from the heat and allow to stand, covered, for 1 hour to draw out the flavours.

Return the pan to the stove and heat gently. Mix the cornflour (cornstarch) to a smooth paste in a cup with a little cold water. Blend a little of the hot liquid into the mixture, then return to the pan. Bring slowly to the boil, stirring constantly. Simmer for 2–3 minutes. Adjust the seasoning, transfer to a warmed dish and serve.

Note As an alternative to ginger syrup, use honey instead, but increase the amount of ground ginger to 1 × 5ml spoon/1 teaspoon.

Peking Beef

Dendeng Ragi

(Stir-fried Beef and Coconut)

Metric/imperial		American
450g/1 lb	lean beef	1 lb
175g/6 oz	fresh coconut, grated or desiccated (shredded) coconut	2¼ cups
1 × 15ml spoon/ 1 tablespoon	coriander seeds, crushed	1 tablespoon
1 × 5ml spoon/ 1 teaspoon	ground cumin	1 teaspoon
	2 cloves garlic, crushed	
	1 small onion, chopped	
	salt, pepper	
	1 chilli pepper, chopped or 1 × 2.5ml spoon/ ½ teaspoon hot soy sauce	
50ml/2 fl oz	oil	¼ cup
2 × 15ml spoons/ 2 tablespoons	hot water	2 tablespoons
2 × 15ml spoons/ 2 tablespoons	tamarind juice	2 tablespoons

Cut the beef across the grain into thin slices approximately 6 × 3cm/2¼ × 1¼ inches. If using desiccated coconut, soak it with 1 tablespoon water. Pound and mix together the coriander, cumin, garlic, onion, pepper and chilli pepper or hot soy sauce. Heat half the oil in a pan, add the spices and fry. Add the meat slices and continue frying. Add the coconut and hot water, and simmer over a low heat until the moisture has been absorbed. Add the tamarind juice and salt, and simmer, stirring occasionally, until all the moisture has been absorbed or evaporated, and the mixture is as dry as possible.

Heat the remaining oil separately. Pour this into the pan and fry the meat and coconut over a low heat until crisp and brown, turning from time to time to prevent the mixture sticking. Remove the meat from the pan and drain thoroughly on absorbent paper. Mix the fried coconut and meat together and serve with boiled, long-grain rice.

Dendeng Ragi

Cantonese Steak

Metric/imperial		American
600g/1¼ lb	fillet steak in one piece	1¼ lb
3 × 15ml spoons/ 3 tablespoons	oil	3 tablespoons
	1 piece preserved stem ginger, finely chopped	
	½ clove garlic, finely chopped	
	grated rind of ½ orange	
	MARINADE	
20g/¾ oz	cornflour (cornstarch)	3 tablespoons
	baking powder	
1 × 5ml spoon/ 1 teaspoon	ginger syrup (from preserved stem ginger)	1 teaspoon
1 × 5ml spoon/ 1 teaspoon	fresh orange juice	1 teaspoon
1 × 15ml spoon/ 1 tablespoon	Chinese rice wine or dry sherry	1 tablespoon
1 × 15ml spoon/ 1 tablespoon	soy sauce	1 tablespoon
100ml/4 fl oz	water	½ cup
	salt, sugar	
3 × 15ml spoons/ 3 tablespoons	groundnut (peanut) or sesame oil	3 tablespoons
	SAUCE	
2 × 15ml spoons/ 2 tablespoons	tomato ketchup	2 tablespoons
1 × 15ml spoon/ 1 tablespoon	Chinese rice wine or dry sherry	1 tablespoon
2 × 15ml spoons/ 2 tablespoons	water	2 tablespoons
	salt, sugar	
	Worcestershire sauce	
	4 drops Tabasco sauce	
1 × 15ml spoon/ 1 tablespoon	groundnut (peanut) oil	1 tablespoon

Trim off any fat or skin from the steak, pat dry with absorbent paper and carve into 12 thin slices. Pound as flat as possible. To make the marinade, mix the cornflour (cornstarch) and a small pinch of baking powder in a bowl. Add the ginger syrup, orange juice, rice wine or sherry, soy sauce and water. Stir all together and season with salt and sugar. Finally stir in the oil. Rub this marinade into the meat and leave, covered, for 1 hour.

Heat the cooking oil in a large frying pan. Add the ginger, garlic and orange rind to the hot oil, then add the meat. Fry on each side for 2 minutes. Remove from the pan and keep hot on a warmed dish.

To make the sauce, add the tomato ketchup, rice wine or sherry, and water to the hot oil in the pan and mix. Season to taste with salt, sugar, Worcestershire sauce and Tabasco sauce. Put the steaks back in the sauce, stir in the last 15ml spoon/tablespoon of oil, and heat through. Serve immediately on a warmed dish.

Teriyaki Steak

Metric/imperial		American
	4 × 225g/8 oz fillet steaks	
	1 clove garlic	
	salt, pepper	
20g/¾ oz	crystallized (candied) ginger, finely chopped	2 tablespoons
1½ × 15ml spoons/ 1½ tablespoons	brown sugar	1½ tablespoons
150ml/¼ pint	Chinese rice wine or dry sherry	⅔ cup
100ml/4 fl oz	soy sauce	½ cup
150ml/¼ pint	white wine	⅔ cup
	juice of ½ lemon	
	GARNISH	
	4 tomatoes	
50g/2 oz	bean sprouts	½ cup
1 × 15ml spoon/ 1 tablespoon	tomato ketchup	1 tablespoon

Teriyaki is a Japanese seasoning made with soy sauce.

Pat the steaks dry with absorbent paper. Make a marinade as follows: crush the garlic with salt. Mix the garlic and ginger in a shallow bowl with the sugar, rice wine or sherry, soy sauce, white wine and lemon juice. Season with salt and pepper. Put the steaks in the marinade and turn several times. Cover and leave to stand for 12 hours. Turn from time to time during the marinating period.

Cut out any hard parts from the tomato stems. Cut a lid off the tomatoes and scoop out the seeds. Season the inside with salt and pepper. Put the bean sprouts in a pan with the tomato ketchup and heat, stirring, for 5 minutes. Stuff the tomatoes with this mixture.

Drain the steaks well. Put them on a grill (broiler) rack, with the grill (broiler) pan underneath, and grill (broil) 4 minutes each side. Arrange the steaks on warmed plates, garnish with the tomatoes, and serve at once with boiled, long-grain rice.

Teriyaki Steak

Chinese Pepper Steak

Metric/imperial		American
450g/1 lb	rump steak	1 lb
1½ × 15ml spoons/ 1½ tablespoons	cornflour (cornstarch)	1½ tablespoons
2 × 15ml spoons/ 2 tablespoons	Chinese rice wine or dry sherry	2 tablespoons
3 × 15ml spoons/ 3 tablespoons	soy sauce	3 tablespoons
1 × 15ml spoon/ 1 tablespoon	sugar	1 tablespoon
	salt, ground ginger	
	oil for frying	
	2 green peppers, de-seeded and chopped	

Cut the steak into thin slices. Trim off any fat and cut each slice into four pieces. Mix the cornflour (cornstarch), rice wine or sherry, soy sauce, sugar and a pinch of ground ginger in a bowl. Turn the pieces of meat in this marinade, cover, and leave to stand in the refrigerator for 3 hours to absorb the flavours, turning from time to time.

Heat the oil to a very high temperature in a large frying pan. Remove the meat from the marinade, pat it dry with absorbent paper, and fry for 5 minutes, shaking the pan to prevent the meat sticking. Remove from the pan, drain and transfer to a warmed serving dish. Keep warm. Add the peppers to the pan and fry for 5 minutes. Season with salt. Remove from the pan, drain and use to garnish the meat. Serve at once.

Tokyo Steak

Metric/imperial		American
	4 × 150g/5 oz fillet steaks	
1 × 15ml spoon/ 1 tablespoon	green peppercorns	1 tablespoon
2 × 15ml spoons/ 2 tablespoons	sake, Chinese rice wine or dry sherry	2 tablespoons
	salt, ground ginger	
	butter for frying	
300g/11 oz	canned mandarin oranges, drained	scant ¾ lb
20g/¾ oz	butter, cut into flakes	4 teaspoons

Pat the steaks dry with absorbent paper. Mix the peppercorns and sake, rice wine or sherry in a bowl. Season with salt and ground ginger. Rub this mixture well into the steaks. Heat the butter in a frying pan. Add the steaks and fry for 2 minutes each side. Remove the steaks from the pan and arrange them on a grill (broiler) rack, with the grill (broiler) pan underneath to catch the drips. Place the mandarin oranges on top of the steaks and scatter on the flakes of butter. Grill (broil) for 3 minutes. Arrange the steaks on a warmed serving plate and serve with fried bean sprouts, boiled, long-grain rice and sake.

Tokyo Steak

Mongolian Fondue

Metric/imperial		American
850g/1¾ lb	tender beef	1¾ lb
1.5 litres/ 2½ pints	CHICKEN BROTH chicken stock (page 6)	1¾ quarts
	2 carrots, sliced	
	1 leek, sliced	
	¼ celeriac root, chopped	
1 × 15ml spoon/ 1 tablespoon	chopped parsley	1 tablespoon
100ml/4 fl oz	TARTARE SAUCE mayonnaise	½ cup
2 × 15ml spoons/ 2 tablespoons	small capers	2 tablespoons
2 × 15ml spoons/ 2 tablespoons	chopped chives	2 tablespoons
	2 pickled gherkins, finely chopped	
2 × 5ml spoons/ 2 teaspoons	lemon juice	2 teaspoons
2 × 15ml spoons 2 tablespoons	canned evaporated milk	2 tablespoons
	salt, pepper, sugar	
100ml/4 fl oz	KETCHUP SAUCE mayonnaise	½ cup
2 × 15ml spoons/ 2 tablespoons	tomato ketchup	2 tablespoons
1 × 5ml spoon/ 1 teaspoon	Worcestershire sauce	1 teaspoon
	sambal (see Note)	
	curry sauce	
	sugar, salt	

Pat the meat dry with absorbent paper. Cut into thin slices, about the thickness of sliced salami. Bring the chicken stock to the boil on the stove, in the fondue dish. Add the carrots, leek, celeriac and parsley, and simmer for 20 minutes.

To make the tartare sauce, mix the mayonnaise with the capers, chives, gherkins and lemon juice. Stir in the evaporated milk until the sauce is creamy. Season to taste with salt, pepper and a pinch of sugar.

To make the ketchup sauce, mix together the mayonnaise, tomato ketchup and Worcestershire sauce. Stir in a small amount of sambal and a dash of curry sauce. Season to taste with a pinch each of sugar and salt.

Arrange the meat, tartare sauce and ketchup sauce in separate bowls on the table. Place the chicken broth, simmering gently in the fondue dish, over its flame on the table. As the broth evaporates, top it up with boiling water. Each guest wraps a slice of meat round his fondue fork, dips it into the simmering broth, and leaves it there for at least 1 minute to cook the beef through. The meat is then dipped into the sauces and eaten. Serve with boiled, long-grain rice.
Note Sambal is an Indonesian relish, available ready-made.

Chinese Fondue

Metric/imperial		American
850g/1¾ lb	fillet steak (or use half each pork and veal fillet)	1¾ lb
1 litre/1¾ pints	good beef stock	1 quart
2 × 15ml spoons/ 2 tablespoons	white wine or whisky	2 tablespoons
1 × 15ml spoon/ 1 tablespoon	soy sauce	1 tablespoon

Remove all fat and skin from the meat. Cut into thin slices, about the thickness of sliced salami, and arrange on plates in individual portions. Bring the stock to the boil on the stove in the fondue dish. Flavour it with the white wine or whisky, and soy sauce. Put the fondue dish over its flame in the centre of the table. Each guest wraps a slice of meat round his fondue fork, dips it into the boiling stock and lets it cook for 1 minute. The meat is then dipped into various spicy accompaniments and sauces (see below) before being eaten. When all the meat has been eaten, the stock in which it was cooked is poured into small cups and drunk as a soup.

Good accompaniments to a Chinese fondue are well-flavoured sauces such as a curry-flavoured mayonnaise, rémoulade sauce, apple and horseradish cream, fruits in mustard pickle, small pickled onions and sweet-and-sour gherkins. They can be bought ready-prepared or made at home.

Sate Bali

Metric/imperial		American
	4 shallots, chopped	
	3 cloves garlic, crushed	
	1 piece lemon grass (optional)	
	1 small piece root ginger, chopped	
1 × 5ml spoon/ 1 teaspoon	ground coriander	1 teaspoon
1 × 5ml spoon/ 1 teaspoon	belacan (prawn paste)	1 teaspoon
1 × 5ml spoon/ 1 teaspoon	tamarind pulp or 1 date, finely chopped	1 teaspoon
	½ chilli pepper, finely chopped or 1 × 2.5ml spoon/ ½ teaspoon chilli sauce	
1 × 2.5ml spoon/ ½ teaspoon	turmeric or curry powder	½ teaspoon
2 × 5ml spoons/ 2 teaspoons	salt	2 teaspoons
	juice of ½ lemon	
250g/9 oz	pork fillet, cubed	generous ½ lb
250g/9 oz	boneless lamb, cubed	generous ½ lb
2 × 15ml spoons/ 2 tablespoons	oil	2 tablespoons
2 × 15ml spoons/ 2 tablespoons	coconut milk	2 tablespoons
	butter	
1 × 15ml spoon/ 1 tablespoon	soy sauce	1 tablespoon

Pound and mix together the shallots, garlic, lemon grass, ginger, coriander, belacan, tamarind or date, chilli, turmeric or curry powder and salt. Stir in the lemon juice. Add the meat, stir well, and leave to marinate for at least 1 hour. Remove the meat from the marinade and drain, reserving the marinade. Thread the meat on to small skewers (about 5 pieces to a skewer) and brush with oil. Barbecue over a charcoal fire, or grill (broil) on a rack with the grill (broiler) pan underneath to catch the drips, turning from time to time. Baste with the oil during cooking.

The leftover marinade can be used as an accompanying sauce, thinned with the coconut milk and, if necessary, a knob of butter and the soy sauce. This mixture is heated up and served separately in a small bowl.

Ho Go

(Chinese Hotpot)

SERVES 6

Metric/imperial		American
	6 eggs	
80ml/3 fl oz	soy sauce	6 tablespoons
	4 boneless chicken breasts, skinned	
	4 chicken livers	
225g/8 oz	fillet steak	½ lb
225g/8 oz	pork fillet	½ lb
300g/11 oz	bamboo shoots	2 cups
	2 leeks, sliced	
225g/8 oz	prawns (shrimp), peeled	½ lb
225g/8 oz	fresh mushrooms, sliced	½ lb
225g/8 oz	fresh bean sprouts	½ lb
1.5 litres/ 2½ pints	chicken stock (page 6)	1¼ quarts

Whisk together the eggs and soy sauce; divide this mixture between six bowls, placing one at each place setting. Cut the chicken breasts and livers into thin strips. Cut the fillet steak and pork fillet into thin slices the thickness of sliced salami. Cut the bamboo shoots into thin strips. Blanch the leeks in hot water and drain. Put these ingredients, and the prawns (shrimp), mushrooms and bean sprouts, into separate bowls and arrange on the table. Heat the chicken stock on the stove in a fondue dish. When it has come to the boil, place the dish over its flame in the centre of the table.

Each guest helps himself to a selection of raw ingredients from the bowls on the table. Using a fondue fork, he then spears several ingredients and dips them into the boiling stock until they are cooked, then dips them into his bowl of egg and soy sauce before eating. When all the meat and vegetables have been eaten, the stock is poured into the bowls containing the remains of the egg and soy sauce, stirred around and drunk as soup.

Sate Padang

Metric/imperial		American
1 × 5ml spoon/ 1 teaspoon	salt	1 teaspoon
450g/1 lb	beef, cubed	1 lb
	1 onion, chopped	
	2 cloves garlic, chopped	
1 × 5ml spoon/ 1 teaspoon	chilli sauce	1 teaspoon
	1 small piece root ginger, chopped	
1 × 2.5ml spoon/ ½ teaspoon	ground galingale (optional)	½ teaspoon
1 × 2.5ml spoon/ ½ teaspoon	pepper	½ teaspoon
1 × 5ml spoon/ 1 teaspoon	turmeric	1 teaspoon
1 × 2.5ml spoon/ ½ teaspoon	ground coriander	½ teaspoon
1 × 5ml spoon/ 1 teaspoon	ground cumin	1 teaspoon
	2 pieces lemon grass (optional)	
2 × 15ml spoons/ 2 tablespoons	rice flour or cornflour (cornstarch)	2 tablespoons

Rub the salt into the meat cubes. Pound and mix together the onion, garlic, chilli sauce, ginger, galingale, pepper, turmeric, coriander and cumin. Put three quarters of this spicy marinade into a saucepan. Add the meat and stir. Allow to stand for 15 minutes so that the meat absorbs all the flavours, then add just enough water to cover the meat. Bring to the boil, reduce the heat, add the lemon grass and simmer, with the pan partly covered, until the meat is nearly cooked but still firm.

Remove the meat from the pan and allow to drain. Add the remaining marinade to the pan and continue to simmer. Carefully thread the pieces of meat on to small kebab skewers and finish cooking by grilling (broiling), preferably over charcoal, until well browned. Baste occasionally with the marinade during the cooking.

Mix the rice flour or cornflour (cornstarch) to a smooth paste in a cup with a little cold water. Blend a little of the hot marinade into the mixture, then return to the pan. Bring slowly to the boil, stirring constantly. Simmer for 2–3 minutes to allow the flour to cook through. Arrange the meat on warmed plates, pour the sauce over and serve as part of a Malaysian or Indonesian-style dinner.

Note Great care should be taken not to let the meat get too tender at the braising stage, as it still has to be grilled (broiled).

Chu-bua-buo

(Oriental Fondue)

SERVES 6

Metric/imperial		American
225g/8 oz	pork fillet	½ lb
225g/8 oz	fillet of beef	½ lb
225g/8 oz	calves' liver	½ lb
225g/8 oz	fillets of sole	½ lb
175g/6 oz	chicken breast, skinned and boned	6 oz
450g/1 lb	celery	1 lb
100g/4 oz	transparent noodles	¼ lb
2 × 15ml spoons/ 2 tablespoons	soy sauce	2 tablespoons
2 × 15ml spoons/ 2 tablespoons	oil	2 tablespoons
2 × 15ml spoons/ 2 tablespoons	Chinese rice wine or dry sherry	2 tablespoons
	3 eggs	
225g/8 oz	spinach, washed and picked over	½ lb
2 litres/ 3½ pints	chicken stock (page 6)	2 quarts

Pat the pork, beef, liver, fish and chicken dry with absorbent paper. Place in the freezing compartment of the refrigerator for 30 minutes; this will enable you to cut them very thin with a sharp knife. Cut them into strips 8 × 2cm/3¼ × ¾ inch. Cut the celery into similar-sized strips, blanch in boiling water for 4 minutes, drain and pat dry. Soak the noodles for 30 minutes in warm water. Drain and cut into pieces 10cm/4 inches long.

Make a sauce as follows: beat together the soy sauce, oil, rice wine or sherry and eggs. Divide the sauce between 6 small bowls. Arrange the meat, fish, noodles, celery and spinach in individual bowls and place on the table. Heat the chicken stock to boiling point in a fondue dish on the stove, then stand over its flame in the centre of the table.

Lay the table with a fondue fork and an empty bowl for each person. Each guest puts some meat in his bowl, spears it with his fork and cooks it for 1 minute in the chicken stock. When it is done, he dips it into his sauce and eats it. The meat and fish are eaten first, then the noodles and vegetables are cooked for 1 minute in the remaining stock.

RICE, NOODLES AND DUMPLINGS

Special Fried Rice

Metric/imperial		American
200g/7 oz	long-grain rice	1 cup
200g/7 oz	cooked ham	scant ½ lb
3 × 15ml spoons/ 3 tablespoons	oil	3 tablespoons
150g/5 oz	shrimps, peeled	5 oz
2 × 15ml spoons/ 2 tablespoons	soy sauce	2 tablespoons
	1 leek, sliced	
	4 eggs, beaten	
	salt, pepper	

The cookery of North China is famous for noodle dishes. Noodles are considered a symbol of longevity in China – hence why they are nearly all very long. The types usually found in oriental supermarkets in Europe are transparent noodles, made of pea-starch or rice flour, and Chinese noodles made of wheat flour. Rice dishes are more common in South China. Long-grain rice is most often used.

Bring a pan of salted water to the boil. Add the rice and cook at a fast boil for 10 minutes. Drain in a sieve, rinse under the cold tap and drain again. Cut the ham into strips. Heat the oil in a pan. Fry the ham and shrimps for 5 minutes, stirring all the time. Add the rice and soy sauce and fry for another 5 minutes. Add the leek and fry for a further 5 minutes. Season the beaten eggs and stir into the pan until they scramble. Arrange on a warmed dish and serve.

Special Fried Rice

Indonesian Rijstaffel

SERVES 10

This is the famous national dish of Indonesia, served in top-class restaurants all over the world, and highly praised by gourmets. It comes originally from Java. Rijstaffel is a Dutch word meaning, literally, 'rice table'. Because of the number of different dishes involved, it takes quite some time to prepare. For a special meal you should aim for a mixture of 9 or 10 dishes, some hot and some cold. For an ordinary family meal, you can serve fewer dishes. All the different dishes are arranged on the table and each guest helps himself to whatever he fancies.

To be served cold:

ROASTED COCONUT

Metric/imperial		American
100g/4 oz	coconut, coarsely grated	1⅓ cups
50g/2 oz	peanuts	⅓ cup
1 × 5ml spoon/ 1 teaspoon	sugar	1 teaspoon
	salt	

Mix together in a bowl the coconut, peanuts and sugar. Season to taste with salt. Brown in a hot frying pan for 5 minutes, stirring all the time. Put into a small bowl for serving.

ROASTED PEANUTS

Metric/imperial		American
225g/8 oz	peanuts	1½ cups
	salt	
1 × 15ml spoon/ 1 tablespoon	coconut oil	1 tablespoon

Sprinkle the peanuts with salt. Heat the oil in a frying pan, add the peanuts and fry over a moderate heat for 10 minutes, until golden brown. Put into a small bowl for serving.

KROEPOEK

oil for deep frying	
1 packet kroepoek	

Kroepoek is pounded dried shrimp mixed with tapioca flour, and pressed into dry slices. It can be bought in oriental food shops. The slices are about 4cm/1½ inches in size, and swell up to twice that size in the hot fat.

    Heat the oil in a large pan. Deep fry the pieces of kroepoek, 2 or 3 at a time, but do not let them brown or they will lose their flavour. Arrange on a dish for serving.
Note The following should also be served cold. You will need 2–3 kinds of sambal (Indonesian relishes made of pounded or crushed ingredients). For instance, sambal oelek (very hot), sambal badjak and sambal goreng. Other suitable accompaniments are small pickled gherkins, sliced cooked beetroot (beets), small pickled onions, and canned sweet-and-sour ginger. There should also be 1 hard-boiled egg per person, cut into slices, and slices of cold roast chicken. The eggs and chicken slices are covered with a sambal sauce (see recipe below).

SAMBAL SAUCE

Metric/imperial		American
	½ clove garlic	
	salt	
3 × 15ml spoons/ 3 tablespoons	coconut oil	3 tablespoons
	1 shallot, chopped	
	2 almonds, chopped	
	2 small red peppers, de-seeded and chopped	
	¼ bay leaf	
150ml/¼ pint	tamarind juice or strong chicken stock	⅔ cup
150ml/¼ pint	coconut milk	⅔ cup
	sugar	

Crush the garlic with salt. Heat the oil in a pan, add the shallot, garlic, almonds and peppers, and fry for 5 minutes, until brown. Add the bay leaf, tamarind juice or chicken stock, and coconut milk. Bring to the boil, stirring, and continue to boil for 1 minute. Season to taste with salt and sugar. Allow to cool. Arrange the hard-boiled egg and chicken slices on a plate; pour the sauce over before serving.

To be served hot:

CURRY SOUP

Metric/imperial		American
	1 clove garlic	
	salt, ground coriander	
3 × 15ml spoons/ 3 tablespoons	oil	3 tablespoons
	3 small red peppers, de-seeded and chopped	
	3 small green peppers, de-seeded and chopped	
	5 shallots, chopped	
1 × 5ml spoon/ 1 teaspoon	ground cumin	1 teaspoon
1 × 5ml spoon/ 1 teaspoon	ground ginger	1 teaspoon
1kg/2 lb	chicken, skinned and boned	2 lb
40g/1½ oz	butter	3 tablespoons
450g/1 lb	celery, chopped	4 cups
	1 bay leaf	
1.5 litres/ 2½ pints	hot water	1¾ quarts
	juice of 1 lemon	

Crush the garlic with salt. Heat the oil in a pan. Add the peppers, shallots, garlic, cumin and a pinch of coriander, and fry gently for a few minutes, stirring. Add the ginger. Fry for 15 minutes, until brown. Put the mixture through a sieve or liquidize it, and set aside. Cut the chicken into pieces about 4cm/1½ inches in size. Heat the butter in a large pan, add the chicken and fry gently on all sides for 15 minutes, until browned. Add the celery, bay leaf, reserved purée and water, and simmer for 30 minutes, until the chicken is tender. Season to taste with the lemon juice and salt, remove the bay leaf, and keep warm until needed.

Note The original version of this recipe uses an Indian vegetable called seré instead of the celery; you may be able to find it canned in shops specializing in exotic foods.

INDIAN CHICKEN CURRY

Metric/imperial		American
1.5kg/3 lb	chicken	3 lb
50g/2 oz	butter	4 tablespoons
	1 onion, chopped	
2 × 5ml spoons/ 2 teaspoons	flour	2 teaspoons
1 × 15ml spoon/ 1 tablespoon	curry powder	1 tablespoon
2 × 5ml spoons/ 2 teaspoons	curry paste	2 teaspoons
450ml/¾ pint	chicken stock (page 6)	2 cups
	1 apple, peeled and chopped	
2 × 5ml spoons/ 2 teaspoons	mango chutney	2 teaspoons
1 × 15ml spoon/ 1 tablespoon	lemon juice	1 tablespoon
	salt, pepper	
25g/1 oz	sultanas (golden raisins)	3 tablespoons
25g/1 oz	blanched almonds	2½ tablespoons
2 × 5ml spoons 2 teaspoons	desiccated (shredded) coconut	2 teaspoons
2 × 15ml spoons/ 2 tablespoons	cream	2 tablespoons
	1 banana, sliced	

Divide the chicken into neat portions. Melt the butter in a large pan, add the chicken and fry until lightly browned. Remove from the pan, drain and keep warm. Add the onion and fry until golden. Add the flour, curry powder and curry paste and fry well, stirring occasionally. Stir in the stock and bring to the boil. Return the chicken to the pan and add all the remaining ingredients except the cream and banana. (The coconut should be tied in muslin and removed after 15 minutes.) Simmer gently for 1¼ hours, adding a little more stock if necessary.

Remove the chicken pieces from the pan, drain and keep warm. Stir the cream into the sauce and set aside. Before serving, re-heat the sauce and pour over the chicken pieces. Garnish with banana slices.

SATCH

Small meat kebabs, prepared according to the recipe for Sate Bali (page 53). Keep warm until needed.

MEAT DUMPLINGS

Metric/imperial		American
	1 clove garlic	
	salt	
450g/1 lb	minced (ground) beef	1 lb
5 × 15ml spoons/ 5 tablespoons	cold water	⅓ cup
1 × 5ml spoon/ 1 teaspoon	ground coriander	1 teaspoon
1 × 5ml spoon/ 1 teaspoon	ground cumin	1 teaspoon
	1 onion, chopped	
	pinch of dried mint	
50ml/2 fl oz	coconut oil	¼ cup
300ml/½ pint	hot meat stock (page 7)	1¼ cups
1 × 5ml spoon/ 1 teaspoon	curry powder	1 teaspoon
1 × 15ml spoon/ 1 tablespoon	cornflour (cornstarch)	1 tablespoon

Crush the garlic with salt. Mix the beef and water together in a pan until thick. Heat gently for 5 minutes, stirring. Remove from the heat, add the coriander, cumin, onion, garlic and dried mint, and mix well. Knead into a doughy consistency. Season with salt if desired. Wet your hands and form the mixture into small dumplings (2cm/¾ inch). Heat the coconut oil in a pan, and fry the dumplings for 10 minutes until browned. Transfer to a dish and keep warm.

To make the sauce, add the stock to the remaining oil and meat juices in the pan. Stir in the curry powder. Mix the cornflour (cornstarch) to a smooth paste in a cup with a little cold water. Blend in a little of the hot liquid, then return to the pan. Bring slowly to the boil, stirring constantly. Simmer for 2–3 minutes to allow the flour to cook through. Season and set aside. Just before serving, re-heat the sauce and pour over the dumplings.

FRIED SHRIMPS

Metric/imperial		American
450g/1 lb	shrimps or prawns, peeled	1 lb
	2 egg yolks	
40g/1½ oz	breadcrumbs	½ cup
5 × 15ml spoons/ 5 tablespoons	coconut oil	⅓ cup

Butterfly the shrimps or prawns, spread out flat, coat with egg yolk and then with breadcrumbs. Heat the oil and fry them for 10 minutes, until brown. Keep warm until needed.

Note You should also serve hot a large bowl of boiled, long-grain rice and a bowl of banana slices fried in butter.

Overleaf: Indonesian Rijstaffel

Javanese Rice

Metric/imperial		American
225g/8 oz	long-grain rice	1 cup
50g/2 oz	butter or margarine	4 tablespoons
	4 chicken legs, skinned, boned and sliced	
200g/7 oz	shrimps, peeled	scant ½ lb
	2 red peppers, de-seeded and chopped	
	1 piece preserved stem ginger	
50g/2 oz	flaked (slivered) almonds	½ cup
1 × 5ml spoon/ 1 teaspoon	curry powder	1 teaspoon
	pinch of ground ginger	
	1 small jar Chinese or Italian fruits pickled with mustard, drained	

Wash the rice thoroughly under the cold tap and drain. Bring a pan of salted water to the boil, add the rice and simmer gently for 15 minutes.

Meanwhile melt the butter or margarine in a large pan. Fry the chicken slices on all sides for 5 minutes, until lightly browned. Add the shrimps and peppers and continue frying for another 5 minutes, stirring all the time. Cut the piece of ginger into quarters and then into very thin slices. Add to the pan with the almonds and continue frying for a further 3 minutes. Drain the rice in a sieve, rinse with warm water and drain again. Add the rice to the pan and heat through, stirring. Season with the curry powder and a small pinch of ground ginger. Stir in the fruits and serve.

Javanese Rice

Indonesian Rice Salad

Metric/imperial		American
100g/4 oz	long-grain rice	½ cup
2 × 15ml spoons/ 2 tablespoons	oil	2 tablespoons
	1 onion, finely chopped	
1 × 15ml spoon/ 1 tablespoon	curry powder	1 tablespoon
250g/9 oz	cold roast chicken, cut into strips	1¾ cups
	1 apple, peeled, cored and chopped	
	1 orange, divided into segments, pith and skin removed, and chopped	
	1 banana, peeled and chopped	
	½ fennel bulk, trimmed and chopped	
	1 red pepper, de-seeded and chopped	
	1 chilli pepper, de-seeded and chopped	
	1 piece preserved stem ginger, chopped	
	DRESSING juice of 1 lemon	
50ml/2 fl oz	tomato ketchup	¼ cup
1–2 × 5ml spoons/ 1–2 teaspoons	Pernod	1–2 teaspoons
50ml/2 fl oz	mayonnaise	¼ cup
2 × 15ml spoons/ 2 tablespoons	soured cream	2 tablespoons
50g/2 oz	**GARNISH** flaked (slivered) almonds, toasted	½ cup
	1 orange, sliced	
	8 maraschino cherries	

Bring a pan of salted water to the boil. Add the rice, reduce the heat and simmer for 15 minutes, until tender. Drain the rice, rinse under the cold tap, and drain again thoroughly.

Heat the oil in a pan and fry the onion gently for 5 minutes, until soft. Remove the pan from the heat and stir in the curry powder and rice. Turn the contents of the pan into a bowl, and mix in the chicken, fruit, vegetables and ginger.

To make the dressing, mix the lemon juice, tomato ketchup, Pernod, mayonnaise and cream in a bowl. Pour three quarters of the dressing on to the rice mixture and mix in thoroughly. Allow to stand for 1 hour.

To serve, arrange the rice salad in 4 separate bowls. Pour the remaining dressing over the 4 salads, and garnish with the nuts, orange slices and cherries.

Indonesian Rice Salad

Nasi Goreng

(Indonesian Fried Rice)

SERVES 8

Metric/imperial		American
600g/1¼ lb	boiling chicken, quartered	1¼ lb
1 litre/1¾ pints	water	1 quart
	salt, pepper	
400g/14 oz	long-grain rice	1¾ cups
	1 red pepper, de-seeded	
100ml/4 fl oz	oil	½ cup
	4 onions, chopped	
	3 cloves garlic, chopped	
300g/11 oz	canned crabmeat, drained	scant ¾ lb
250g/9 oz	cooked ham	generous ½ lb
600g/1¼ lb	prawns (shrimp), peeled	1¼ lb
	3 eggs, beaten	
1 × 5ml spoon/ 1 teaspoon	sambal oelek (an Indonesian relish)	1 teaspoon
	curry powder, ground ginger, ground cumin, ground coriander, ground nutmeg, powdered saffron (or turmeric)	

Place the chicken pieces in a large, heavy saucepan. Cover generously with water and bring to the boil. Skim off any froth or bits which rise to the surface. Reduce the heat and simmer, covered, for 1 hour or until tender.

Remove the chicken pieces from the stock and allow to cool. Then remove the skin and bones from the chicken, cut the flesh into small pieces and set aside. Put the chicken stock in a pan, add the 1 litre/1¾ pints/1 quart water and a pinch of salt, and bring to the boil. Meanwhile, wash the rice until the water runs clear. Add the rice to the boiling liquid and simmer for 12 minutes over a low heat, until the rice grains have swelled but are not completely cooked. Drain in a sieve, pour warm water over the rice to rinse it, and drain again. Cut the pepper into narrow strips.

Heat 80 ml/3 fl oz/6 tablespoons of the oil in a large pan. Add the onions, garlic and pepper and stew gently for 5 minutes. Add the rice. Continue cooking very gently for 10 minutes, stirring frequently. Remove any hard pieces from the crabmeat. Cut the ham into strips. Add the crabmeat, ham, prawns (shrimp) and chicken to the pan and mix. Heat the remaining oil in another pan. Add the eggs and scramble, stirring. Mix the sambal oelek and spices to taste in a cup with a little water. Add to the rice mixture with the scrambled egg and stir. Leave over a very low heat for 10 minutes, stirring occasionally.

Transfer the mixture to a warmed dish and serve with a selection of spicy sauces and side dishes. These can be prepared beforehand or bought ready-made. Suitable accompaniments would be: sweet peppers in an oil and vinegar dressing; pineapple chunks; pickled cucumber; chilli sauce; mixed pickles; mustard pickles; mango chutney; tomato ketchup; soy sauce; fried sliced banana; crystallized (candied) ginger; roasted peanuts or cashew nuts and any Indonesian relish available.

Bami Kuah

(Fried Noodles with Chicken and Pork)

Metric/imperial		American
225g/8 oz	Chinese egg noodles	½ lb
3½ × 15ml spoons/ 3½ tablespoons	oil	3½ tablespoons
750g/1½ lb	chicken	1½ lb
250g/9 oz	pork	generous ½ lb
	salt, pepper	
1 litre/ 1¾ pints	water	1 quart
50g/2 oz	fresh button mushrooms	¾ cup
	1 clove garlic, crushed	
1 × 5ml spoon/ 1 teaspoon	finely chopped root ginger	1 teaspoon
	1 small leek, sliced	
1 × 15ml spoon/ 1 tablespoon	finely chopped celery	1 tablespoon
1 × 15ml spoon/ 1 tablespoon	soy sauce	1 tablespoon
3 × 15ml spoons/ 3 tablespoons	crisply fried onions	3 tablespoons
3 × 15ml spoons/ 3 tablespoons	chopped chives	3 tablespoons

Cook the noodles until tender as indicated on the packet. Drain in a sieve, rinse under the cold tap and drain again thoroughly, then turn them in 1½ × 5ml spoons/1½ teaspoons of the oil. Put the chicken and pork in a saucepan and season. Add the water and bring to the boil. Skim the liquid, reduce the heat, cover the pan and leave to simmer for 15–20 minutes. Remove the chicken and pork from the saucepan, skin and bone the chicken, then slice both the chicken and pork thinly. Strain the stock and keep hot.

Heat 2 × 15ml spoons/2 tablespoons of the oil in a pan and fry the mushrooms for 1 minute. Add the chicken and pork and turn in the hot oil for a further minute. Remove everything from the pan and keep hot. Heat the remaining oil in the pan and fry the garlic and ginger for 1 minute. Remove and add to the other ingredients being kept hot, then fry the leek and celery in the oil for 2 to 3 minutes. Return the chicken, pork, mushrooms, garlic and ginger to the pan, pour over the hot stock and soy sauce. Add a little more salt to taste. Stir in the noodles and heat through. Serve in large bowls garnished with the onions and chives.

Chicken Chow Mein

Metric/imperial		American
	1 small green pepper, de-seeded	
	1 small red pepper, de-seeded	
40g/1½ oz	butter	3 tablespoons
	1 small onion, chopped	
	2 sticks celery, chopped	
1½ × 15ml spoons/ 1½ tablespoons	flour	1½ tablespoons
300ml/½ pint	hot chicken stock (page 6)	1¼ cups
2 × 15ml spoons/ 2 tablespoons	soy sauce	2 tablespoons
	pepper	
150g/5 oz	mushrooms, sliced	2 cups
225g/8 oz	cooked chicken breast, chopped	1½ cups
225g/8 oz	broad Chinese noodles	½ lb
	oil for frying	
100g/4 oz	flaked (slivered) almonds, fried in butter and salted	1 cup

Cut the peppers into thin strips and blanch in boiling water for 5 minutes. Remove and drain. Melt 25g/1 oz/2 US tablespoons of the butter in a pan, add the onion and celery, and fry lightly for 2 minutes. Sprinkle the flour over, add the stock, bring to the boil and simmer for 10 minutes, until the vegetables are just tender. Season with the soy sauce and pepper. Add the pepper strips, mushrooms and chicken breast. Cover the pan and simmer gently for 15 minutes.

Bring a pan of salted water to the boil, add the noodles and simmer for 15 minutes. Drain, rinse with cold water and drain again. Set aside one third of the noodles. Add the remaining butter to the rest and put into a warmed serving dish. Cover and keep warm.

Cut the remaining noodles, which must be very well drained, into pieces. Heat the oil in a frying pan and fry the noodles until golden yellow. Drain on absorbent paper. Pour the chicken sauce over the buttered noodles and sprinkle the fried noodles and salted almonds on top. Alternatively, the chicken sauce, buttered noodles, fried noodles and salted almonds can all be served separately.

Chicken Chow Mein

Far Eastern Rice Platter

Metric/imperial		American
350g/12 oz	long-grain rice	1½ cups
100g/4 oz	butter	½ cup
50g/2 oz	sultanas (golden raisins)	⅓ cup
350g/12 oz	pork fillet	¾ lb
	salt, pepper	
50ml/2 fl oz	oil	¼ cup
250g/9 oz	fillets of sole	generous ½ lb
5 × 15ml spoons/ 5 tablespoons	lemon juice	⅓ cup
250g/9 oz	boiled shrimps, peeled	generous ½ lb
200g/7 oz	canned pineapple pieces, drained	scant ½ lb
200g/7 oz	canned red peppers, drained and chopped	scant ½ lb
150g/5 oz	black (ripe) olives, stoned and sliced	1 cup
225g/8 oz	fresh mushrooms, quartered	½ lb
	2 bananas	
100g/4 oz	flaked (slivered) almonds, toasted	1 cup
	CURRY SAUCE	
60g/2½ oz	butter	5 tablespoons
40g/1½ oz	flour	6 tablespoons
500ml/17 fl oz	hot stock	2 cups
4 × 15ml spoons/ 4 tablespoons	curry powder	4 tablespoons
150ml/¼ pint	white wine	⅔ cup
	salt, pepper, sugar	
2 × 15ml spoons/ 2 tablespoons	single (light) cream	2 tablespoons

Bring a pan of salted water to the boil, add the rice and boil for 10 minutes, until just tender. Drain, rinse, and drain again thoroughly. Grease a baking sheet with butter and spread the rice out on it. Cut 25g/1 oz/2 US tablespoons of the butter into flakes and arrange them on top of the rice. Bake at 180°C/350°F/Gas 4 for 15 minutes until all the moisture has steamed away.

Meanwhile soak the sultanas (golden raisins) in hot water, and make the curry sauce as follows. Melt the butter in a pan. Add the flour, and stir until smooth. Still stirring, add the stock, curry powder and wine. Season with salt, pepper and a pinch of sugar. Bring to the boil, remove the pan from the heat, and stir in the cream. Adjust seasoning, keep the sauce hot.

Cut the pork first into thin slices, and then into narrow strips of even size. Season with salt and pepper. Heat 2 × 15ml spoons/2 tablespoons oil in a pan, and fry the pork strips on all sides for 8 minutes. Remove and keep hot.

Sprinkle the sole fillets with 4 × 15ml spoons/4 tablespoons of the lemon juice and a little salt. Heat the remaining oil in another pan and fry the sole fillets for 5 minutes each side. Add the shrimps and heat through. Remove and keep hot.

Drain the sultanas (golden raisins) thoroughly. Melt 40g/1½ oz/3 US tablespoons of the butter in a pan. Add the sultanas (golden raisins), pineapple pieces, red peppers and olives to the pan, and fry gently, stirring, until heated through thoroughly. Remove and keep hot.

Melt 20g/¾ oz/1½ US tablespoons of the butter in a pan and fry the mushrooms for 10 minutes. Season with the remaining lemon juice, salt and pepper. Remove and keep hot.

Finally, cut each banana in half widthways, and then cut each piece in half lengthways. Melt the remaining butter in a pan, and fry the banana pieces for 10 minutes, until golden-brown. Turn the banana pieces frequently and baste them with the butter in the pan.

Now assemble the dish. Spread the rice out on a large, flat serving dish. Arrange the pork, the sole and shrimp mixture, the sultana (golden raisin), pineapple, pepper and olive mixture, the mushrooms, and the fried bananas on top of the rice. Scatter on the nuts. Serve the curry sauce separately.

Chop Suey

Metric/imperial		American
450g/1 lb	lean pork	1 lb
2 × 15ml spoons/ 2 tablespoons	Chinese rice wine or dry sherry	2 tablespoons
50ml/2 fl oz	soy sauce	$\frac{1}{4}$ cup
	salt, pepper, ground ginger	
50g/2 oz	transparent noodles	2 oz
50g/2 oz	celery	$\frac{1}{3}$ cup
1 × 15ml spoon/ 1 tablespoon	dried Chinese mushrooms	1 tablespoon
75g/3 oz	bamboo shoots	$\frac{1}{2}$ cup
100ml/4 fl oz	groundnut (peanut) oil	$\frac{1}{2}$ cup
	2 onions, chopped	
150g/5 oz	bean sprouts	1$\frac{1}{2}$ cups
100g/4 oz	fresh mushrooms, sliced	$\frac{1}{4}$ lb
1 × 5ml spoon/ 1 teaspoon	sugar	1 teaspoon
1$\frac{1}{2}$ × 15ml spoons/ 1$\frac{1}{2}$ tablespoons	cornflour (cornstarch)	1$\frac{1}{2}$ tablespoons
50ml/2 fl oz	dry sherry	$\frac{1}{4}$ cup

Cut the pork into thin strips. Mix 2 × 15ml spoons/ 2 tablespoons rice wine or sherry and half the soy sauce in a bowl. Season with salt, pepper and a pinch of ground ginger. Add the pork strips to the marinade, cover and allow to stand for 1 hour. Meanwhile break up the noodles into small pieces. Bring a pan of lightly salted water to the boil, add the noodles and simmer for 5 minutes. Rinse under the cold tap, drain and set aside. Cut the celery into short strips and blanch for 5 minutes in boiling, lightly salted water. Remove and drain. Soak the dried mushrooms in warm water for 30 minutes, drain and cut into fairly large pieces. Cut the bamboo shoots into strips.

Put the oil in a large frying pan and heat it until very hot. Remove the pork from the marinade, drain well and fry in the oil for 2 minutes. Remove and keep warm. Add the onions, bamboo shoots, bean sprouts, dried and fresh mushrooms. Fry for 3 minutes. Mix in the pork, celery and noodles. Season with the remaining soy sauce and the sugar. Simmer for another 3 minutes, stirring gently.

Mix the cornflour (cornstarch) to a smooth paste in a cup with the sherry. Add to the pan and bring slowly to the boil, stirring constantly. Simmer for 2–3 minutes to allow the flour to cook through. Adjust the seasoning and serve at once with boiled, long-grain rice.

Chinese Steamed Rolls

Chinese Steamed Rolls

To make the dough, cream the fresh yeast with half the sugar and a little of the water, then add the remaining water. (If using dried yeast, dissolve the sugar in the water, sprinkle on the yeast and stir well.) Leave to stand in a warm place for about 10 minutes.

Meanwhile sift the flour into a bowl. Make a well in the centre and pour in the yeast mixture. Working from the outside in, knead to a soft dough which leaves the sides of the bowl clean (about 10 minutes). Add a little more flour if necessary. Allow the dough to stand in a warm place, covered with a clean cloth, until it has doubled in size.

Meanwhile, make the filling. Heat the oil in a pan. Add the onion and garlic and fry until golden. Add the pork and stir over high heat until thoroughly heated through. Add the soy sauce, rice wine or sherry and remaining sugar and mix in well. Mix the cornflour (cornstarch) to a smooth paste in a cup with the water or stock. Stir into the ingredients in the pan until the sauce is thick and shiny. Remove the pan from the heat and allow to cool.

Turn the dough on to a floured surface. Knead again for 1 to 2 minutes to knock out air bubbles. Shape into a sausage 5cm/2 inches thick, and cut into slices 2cm/¾ inch thick. Roll these slices out until they are 7.5–10cm/3–4 inches across. Divide the filling among the dough slices, heaping it up in the centre. Fold the edges upwards so that the filling is completely enclosed, and shape into a ball. Cut circles of aluminium foil or greaseproof (waxed) paper just large enough for the rolls to stand on. Place each roll on a rack inside a steamer, over a pan of boiling water. Steam the rolls 2cm/¾ inch apart, a few at a time, for 15–20 minutes, or until the topsides are shiny and firm. These rolls can be eaten either hot or cold.

Metric/imperial		American
15g/½ oz or 2 × 5ml spoons/ 2 teaspoons	fresh yeast or dry yeast	½ cake compressed or 1½ packages
2 × 15ml spoons/ 2 tablespoons	sugar	2 tablespoons
250ml/8 fl oz	warm water	1 cup
450g/1 lb	flour	4 cups
2 × 15ml spoons/ 2 tablespoons	oil	2 tablespoons
	4 spring onions (scallions) or ½ onion, chopped	
	1 clove garlic, crushed	
450g/1 lb	Chinese roast belly of pork, (page 39), finely shredded	1 lb
2 × 15ml spoons/ 2 tablespoons	soy sauce	2 tablespoons
1½ × 5ml spoons/ 1½ teaspoons	Chinese rice wine or dry sherry	1½ teaspoons
1½ × 15ml spoons/ 1½ tablespoons	cornflour (cornstarch)	1½ tablespoons
3 × 15ml spoons/ 3 tablespoons	water or stock	3 tablespoons

Siu Mai

(Savoury Dumplings)

SERVES 8-10

Metric/imperial		American
	3 dried Chinese mushrooms	
350g/12 oz	lean pork, chopped	$\frac{3}{4}$ lb
100g/4 oz	fat ham, chopped	$\frac{1}{4}$ lb
	1 Dublin Bay prawn (scampi), chopped	
	1 piece (2.5cm/1 inch) bamboo shoot, chopped	
	2 water chestnuts, chopped (optional)	
1 × 15ml spoon/ 1 tablespoon	sake, Chinese rice wine or dry sherry	1 tablespoon
1 × 5ml spoon/ 1 teaspoon	soy sauce	1 teaspoon
	few drops sesame oil	
1 × 2.5ml spoon/ $\frac{1}{2}$ teaspoon	sugar	$\frac{1}{2}$ teaspoon
	1 egg white, beaten	
	salt, pepper	
	10 egg roll or spring roll wrappers	

Soak the mushrooms in hot water for 15–30 minutes, until swollen. Squeeze them dry, remove the stalks and cut the caps into short, thin strips. Mix together all the ingredients except the egg roll wrappers, and set the mixture aside for 1 hour.

Meanwhile take the egg roll wrappers one at a time, and cut out 4 circles 10cm/4 inches in diameter from each, using a pastry cutter or saucer. Divide the filling into 40 equal portions and shape into balls. Place each on a circle of dough. Fold the edges upward over the filling and crimp carefully together. Hold the dumpling a little way above a pastry board and let it drop a few times to flatten the underside and settle the filling. There must be no air between the filling and the dough case. Continue in this way until all the dumplings have been shaped, keeping the egg roll wrappers and the completed dumplings covered with polythene sheets (plastic wrap) as you work.

Steam the dumplings for 20–30 minutes. Place a small piece of aluminium foil under each dumpling to prevent it sticking to the bottom of the steamer. If you only have a small steamer, the dumplings can be steamed in batches, then all heated up together before serving. Serve as an hors d'oeuvre or lunch dish, with an accompanying dip of chilli sauce.

Siu Mai

Sukiyaki

Metric/imperial		American
200g/7 oz	transparent noodles	scant $\frac{1}{2}$ lb
15g/$\frac{1}{2}$ oz	dried Chinese mushrooms	$\frac{3}{4}$ cup
850g/1$\frac{3}{4}$ lb	fillet steak, thinly sliced	1$\frac{3}{4}$ lb
40g/1$\frac{1}{2}$ oz	suet or pork fat	3 tablespoons
400g/14 oz	long-grain rice	1$\frac{3}{4}$ cups
	4 onions	
	4 leeks	
225g/8 oz	white cabbage	$\frac{1}{2}$ lb
450g/1 lb	canned bamboo shoots	1 lb
225g/8 oz	spinach, washed and picked over	$\frac{1}{2}$ lb
225g/8 oz	bean sprouts	$\frac{1}{2}$ lb
	4 egg yolks	
	SAUCE	
300ml/$\frac{1}{2}$ pint	shoyu or soy sauce	1$\frac{1}{4}$ cups
80ml/3 fl oz	sake	6 tablespoons
2 × 5ml spoons/ 2 teaspoons	sugar	2 teaspoons

Put the noodles and dried mushrooms into separate bowls. Pour on boiling water and leave to soak and swell up for 20 minutes, changing the water twice. Arrange the meat on a dish like petals, with the suet or pork fat in the centre.

Bring a pan of salted water to the boil, add the rice and simmer for 15 minutes until tender. Meanwhile cut the onions and leeks into rings. Cut out the cabbage stalk, take the leaves apart and wash and drain them. Halve or quarter the larger leaves. Drain the bamboo shoots, reserving their liquid. Slice thinly. Drain the noodles and mushrooms. Arrange the raw ingredients, including the meat, around a grill (broiler) or gas ring on the table in individual bowls.

To make the sauce, bring the shoyu or soy sauce to the boil in a pan with the sake, sugar and 4 × 15ml spoons/ 4 tablespoons reserved bamboo shoot liquid. Put in a bowl and place on the table. Drain the rice, rinse with boiling water, drain again and place on the table in a bowl.

Sukiyaki is cooked in the following way. Rub round a cooking pan with the suet or fat. Set it over the heat, add a quarter of the meat and fry quickly, stirring. Push the meat to one side of the pan and pour some of the sauce over it. Add a quarter of the remaining ingredients (except the rice and egg) and fry gently, stirring for 3 minutes. The meat and vegetables are then divided between the guests; the cooked vegetables are dipped in the yolk before being eaten. While the first portion of meat and vegetables is being eaten the second is being prepared in the same way until all the ingredients have been cooked. Each guest seasons his food to taste with the sauce and helps himself to rice.

Green tea is the correct drink to accompany Sukiyaki with a cup or bowl of warm sake afterwards.

Overleaf: Sukiyaki

Jo Chon Bau

(Chinese Parcels of Yeast Dough Stuffed with Pork)

Metric/imperial		American
600g/1¼ lb	pork escalopes (boneless pork sliced thinly)	1¼ lb
	2 onions	
	1 leek	
50g/2 oz	butter	4 tablespoons
	salt	
	margarine	
	FIRST MARINADE	
50ml/2 fl oz	tomato ketchup	¼ cup
1 × 15ml spoon/ 1 tablespoon	vinegar	1 tablespoon
1 × 5ml spoon/ 1 teaspoon	mild paprika	1 teaspoon
	3 drops Tabasco (hot pepper) sauce	
1 × 5ml spoon/ 1 teaspoon	curry powder	1 teaspoon
	SECOND MARINADE	
90ml/3½ fl oz	soy sauce	6 tablespoons
1 × 15ml spoon/ 1 tablespoon	Chinese rice wine or dry sherry	1 tablespoon
1 × 15ml spoon/ 1 tablespoon	honey	1 tablespoon
	ground ginger	
	DOUGH	
20g/¾ oz or 1 × 15ml spoon/ 1 tablespoon	fresh yeast or dried yeast	¾ cake compressed or 2 packages
1 × 5ml spoon/ 1 teaspoon	sugar	1 teaspoon
300ml/½ pint	warm water	1¼ cups
400g/14 oz	flour	3½ cups
1 × 2.5ml spoon/ ½ teaspoon	salt	½ teaspoon

Pat the pork escalopes dry with absorbent paper. Trim off any fat.

To make the first marinade, mix together the tomato ketchup, vinegar, paprika, Tabasco sauce and curry powder. Put the meat in a bowl, cover with the marinade, and leave for 10 minutes to absorb the flavours. Meanwhile brush the grill (broiler) rack with oil and put the pan underneath to catch any drips. Remove the escalopes from the marinade, drain and grill (broil) for 10 minutes each side. Alternatively, fry (broil) the meat in a little oil, over gentle heat, for 10 minutes each side.

While the meat is cooking, prepare the second marinade. Warm the soy sauce and rice wine or sherry in a saucepan. Add the honey and stir until dissolved. Season with a pinch of ground ginger and take the pan off the heat. Remove the pork escalopes from the grill (broiler) or frying pan, cut into cubes 1cm/½ inch square, and add to the pan. Cover and leave to stand for 45 minutes.

To make the dough, cream the fresh yeast with the sugar and a little of the water, then add the remaining water. (If using dried yeast, dissolve the sugar in the water, sprinkle on the yeast and stir well.) Leave to stand in a warm place for about 10 minutes.

Meanwhile sift the flour and salt into a bowl. Make a well in the centre and pour in the yeast mixture. Working from the outside in, knead to a soft dough which leaves the sides of the bowl clean (about 10 minutes). Add a little more flour if necessary. Allow the dough to stand in a warm place, covered with a clean cloth, until it doubles in size.

Meanwhile cut the onions into strips. Cut the leek in half lengthways, wash and drain, and cut into pieces 5mm/¼ inch long. Then heat 25g/1 oz 2 US tablespoons of the butter in a frying pan, add the onions and leeks and fry for 5 minutes, stirring. Remove the meat from the second marinade, drain and add to the pan. Season with salt and stew together for 5 minutes.

Turn the dough on to a floured surface. Knead again for 1–2 minutes to knock out air bubbles, then roll out and divide into 8 portions. Form each portion into a circular shape with your hands, put some of the meat mixture into the centre of each circle, and fold the dough into parcels, pressing the edges together well. Melt the remaining butter and paint it over the dough parcels. Cover a roasting grid with foil, grease the foil with margarine, and place the dough parcels on it. Place the grid on a roasting pan partly filled with water. Roast for 20 minutes at 240°C/475°F/ Gas 9. Remove from the oven and serve.

EGG DISHES

Japanese Egg Salad

Metric/imperial		American
200g/7 oz	canned tuna fish, drained	scant ½ lb
200g/7 oz	canned mandarin oranges, drained	scant ½ lb
	4 hard-boiled eggs, sliced	
50g/2 oz	stuffed green olives, sliced	½ cup
2 × 15ml spoons/ 2 tablespoons	oil	2 tablespoons
	juice of 1 lemon	
2 × 15ml spoons/ 2 tablespoons	soy sauce	2 tablespoons
	salt, pepper	
	sugar	
	sprigs parsley	

Flake the fish into a bowl. Add the mandarin oranges, eggs and olives and mix together lightly. To make the dressing, mix together the oil, lemon juice and soy sauce. Season to taste with salt, pepper and a pinch of sugar. Pour over the salad. Stand the salad in the refrigerator, covered, for 10 minutes to absorb the flavours. To serve, divide the salad between four glass dishes and garnish each with a sprig of parsley.

Chinese Tea Eggs

Metric/imperial		American
2 litres/ 3½ pints	water	2 quarts
2 × 15ml spoons/ 2 tablespoons	jasmine tea	2 tablespoons
100g/4 oz	sugar	½ cup
	6 hard-boiled eggs (unshelled)	

Bring the water to the boil in a pan. Add the tea and sugar, and continue to boil for 15 minutes. Strain the liquid, bring back to the boil and allow to simmer gently for 1 hour. Tap the egg shells on all sides to crack evenly, but do not peel them. Put them in the tea and simmer gently for another hour. Take the eggs out of the tea and remove the shells. The egg whites will have an attractive marbled appearance. Serve either hot or cold.

Crayfish Fu Yung

Metric/imperial		American
	juice of ½ lemon	
100g/4 oz	fresh mushrooms, sliced	¼ lb
	2 egg whites	
1 × 5ml spoon/ 1 teaspoon	strong chicken stock	1 teaspoon
	salt, pepper	
150ml/¼ pint	oil	⅔ cup
300g/11 oz	canned crayfish, drained	scant ¾ lb
100g/4 oz	bamboo shoots, thinly sliced	¾ cup
1 × 5ml spoon/ 1 teaspoon	cornflour (cornstarch)	1 teaspoon
1 × 15ml spoon/ 1 tablespoon	water	1 tablespoon
1 × 5ml spoon/ 1 teaspoon	soy sauce	1 teaspoon
2 × 15ml spoons/ 2 tablespoons	Chinese rice wine or dry sherry	2 tablespoons
100g/4 oz	cooked ham, diced	¼ lb

Bring a pan of salted water to the boil. Add the lemon juice and mushrooms and simmer for 5 minutes, until tender. Drain and keep warm.

Mix the egg whites and stock together, season with salt and pepper. Heat the oil in a pan without letting it get too hot. Add the egg white mixture and let it solidify to a smooth, soft consistency. Tip into a sieve and reserve the oil. Pour 3 × 15ml spoons/3 tablespoons oil back into the pan and re-heat. Remove any hard pieces from the crayfish and add the crayfish to the pan with the mushrooms and bamboo shoots. Season with salt and pepper and fry for 2 minutes, then mix in the egg white mixture. Separately, mix the cornflour (cornstarch), water, soy sauce and rice wine or sherry together. Add to the pan and fry over high heat for 30 seconds. Transfer to a warmed dish and garnish with the ham.

Fu Yung Hay

Metric/imperial		American
	2 cloves garlic	
	salt, pepper, ground ginger	
100ml/4 fl oz	oil	½ cup
350g/12 oz	tomatoes, skinned, de-seeded and chopped	¾ lb
1 × 5ml spoon/ 1 teaspoon	sugar	1 teaspoon
2 × 15ml spoons/ 2 tablespoons	soy sauce	2 tablespoons
150g/5 oz	petits pois	1 cup
	butter	
	1 leek, thinly sliced	
	2 onions, thinly sliced	
	8 small, tender sticks celery, thinly sliced	
	8 eggs, beaten	
300g/11 oz	canned crayfish, drained	scant ¾ lb

To make the tomato sauce, crush the garlic with salt. Heat 2 × 15ml spoons/2 tablespoons oil in a pan and fry the garlic for 2 minutes, until pale yellow. Add the tomatoes and cook, stirring, until you have a thick sauce. Season with the sugar, soy sauce and a small pinch of ground ginger, and keep warm.

Bring a pan of salted water to the boil, add the peas, cover, and simmer for 5 minutes, until done. Drain the peas, add a knob of butter and keep warm.

To make the omelets, heat 2 × 15ml spoons/2 tablespoons oil in a pan. Add the leek, onions and celery and fry for 5 minutes, stirring, then stir the vegetable mixture into the eggs. Remove any hard pieces from the crayfish, then stir into the eggs. Season to taste. For each omelet, put 1 × 15ml spoon/1 tablespoon of the remaining oil in a pan. Heat until it is smoking and ladle in a quarter of the egg mixture. Fry over low heat for 5 minutes, shaking the pan from time to time. The omelets should be cooked in quick succession, slid on to warm plates and kept hot. When all the omelets have been cooked, scatter the peas round the edge and serve at once. Serve the tomato sauce separately.

VEGETABLES

Chinese Cabbage

Metric/imperial		American
	2 Chinese cabbages	
20g/¾ oz	butter	1½ tablespoons
	grated nutmeg	

Shred the cabbage leaves, cut them into finger-length pieces, or leave them whole, according to taste. Wash and drain. Bring a pan of salted water to the boil, add the cabbage and simmer for 20–25 minutes, until tender. (The quicker it is cooked the better.) Drain and return to the pan. Add the butter and shake over gentle heat until the butter has melted and the cabbage is coated. Sprinkle with grated nutmeg and serve.

Braised Chinese Cabbage

Metric/imperial		American
	2 Chinese cabbages, quartered	
	salt	
50g/2 oz	streaky bacon, chopped	2 slices
	1 onion, chopped	
300ml/½ pint	stock	1¼ cups
1–2 × 15ml spoons/ 1–2 tablespoons	soy sauce	1–2 tablespoons
1 × 15ml spoon/ 1 tablespoon	chopped parsley	1 tablespoon

Season the cabbages lightly with salt. Fry the bacon in a pan until the fat runs. Add the onion and brown slightly. Add the cabbage and fry quickly, but do not allow to brown. Pour the stock into the pan and simmer for 20 minutes, until the cabbage is tender. Season with soy sauce and more salt if necessary. Transfer to a warmed bowl and serve garnished with parsley.

Braised Chinese Cabbage

Stir-fried Chinese Cabbage

Metric/imperial		American
	1 dried Chinese mushroom	
	2 Chinese cabbages	
2 × 15ml spoons/ 2 tablespoons	oil	2 tablespoons
1½ × 5ml spoons/ 1½ teaspoons	salt	1½ teaspoons
	1 small piece root ginger, finely chopped	
100ml/4 fl oz	chicken stock (page 6)	½ cup
½ × 2.5ml spoon/ ¼ teaspoon	sugar	¼ teaspoon
1 × 15ml spoon/ 1 tablespoon	soy sauce	1 tablespoon
2 × 5ml spoons/ 2 teaspoons	cornflour (cornstarch)	2 teaspoons
1 × 15ml spoon/ 1 tablespoon	water	1 tablespoon

Soak the mushroom in hot water for 15–30 minutes, until swollen. Drain well, remove the stalk and cut the cap into long, thin strips. Cut off the thick stalk from the cabbage. Wash the leaves and shred them into fairly short pieces.

Heat the oil in a wok or other lidded, heavy pan. Add the salt and ginger, and turn in the oil over a high heat for 30 seconds. Add the cabbage and mushroom and fry, turning over continuously, for 1½ minutes. Add the stock, sugar and soy sauce, reduce the heat slightly, place the lid on the pan, and let the ingredients simmer gently for 2 minutes. Meanwhile mix the cornflour (cornstarch) to a smooth paste with the water, then stir this solution into the pan until the sauce thickens and becomes shiny. Serve as an accompaniment to Chinese roast belly of pork (page 39) or other meat dishes.

Chinese Mixed Vegetables

Metric/imperial		American
15g/½ oz	dried Chinese mushrooms	¾ cup
100g/4 oz	white cabbage	1¼ cups
100g/4 oz	carrots, peeled	⅔ cup
100g/4 oz	cucumber, peeled	1 cup
100g/4 oz	bamboo shoots	¾ cup
50ml/2 fl oz	sesame oil	¼ cup
50g/2 oz	peas	⅓ cup
150ml/¼ pint	hot chicken stock (page 6)	⅔ cup
2 × 15ml spoons/ 2 tablespoons	soy sauce	2 tablespoons
	salt, sugar	

Soak the dried mushrooms in warm water for 15–30 minutes, until swollen. Meanwhile, cut the cabbage, carrots, cucumber and bamboo shoots into conveniently sized strips. Drain the mushrooms and cut into pieces. Heat the oil in a frying pan and fry the cabbage, stirring, for 2 minutes. Stir in the mushrooms, carrots, cucumber, bamboo shoots and peas and heat through. Add the stock. Season with the soy sauce and a pinch of salt and sugar. Simmer over low heat for 15 minutes, stirring occasionally. Serve at once.

Chinese Mixed Vegetables

Bebotok

(Cabbage Rolls)

Metric/imperial		American
400g/14 oz	minced (ground) beef	scant 1 lb
2 × 15ml spoons/ 2 tablespoons	onion, finely chopped	2 tablespoons
	1 clove garlic, crushed	
	1 chilli pepper, shredded or 1 × 2.5ml spoon/ ½ teaspoon chilli sauce	
1½ × 15ml spoons/ 1½ tablespoons	ground coriander	1½ tablespoons
1½ × 5ml spoons/ 1½ teaspoons	ground cumin	1½ teaspoons
	6 blanched almonds, chopped	
1 × 2.5ml spoon/ ½ teaspoon	soft brown sugar	½ teaspoon
3 × 15ml spoons/ 3 tablespoons	grated coconut (preferably fresh)	3 tablespoons
1 × 2.5ml spoon/ ½ teaspoon	belacan (prawn paste)	½ teaspoon
1 × 5ml spoon/ 1 teaspoon	salt	1 teaspoon
	1 egg, lightly beaten	
	milk if necessary	
	8–10 large white or green cabbage leaves	

Put all the ingredients except the milk and cabbage leaves into a large bowl, and work together until the mixture becomes tacky and sticks together. Add a little milk if the mixture is too dry. Divide the mixture into 8–10 equal portions, forming each into a slightly flattened ball. Bring a pan of water to the boil, add the cabbage leaves, and simmer until they are soft enough to be folded without breaking. Rinse and drain well. Lay one portion of the filling on each of the leaves, fold the leaves up into a package and secure with wooden cocktail sticks.

Place the rolls in a steamer over a pan of boiling water. Steam the rolls for 20–25 minutes with the lid on, until cooked. Remove from the steamer and serve.

Tung-ku-nidng-jou

(Chinese Mushrooms)

Metric/imperial		American
25g/1 oz	dried Chinese mushrooms	1¼ cups
3 × 15ml spoons/ 3 tablespoons	soy sauce	3 tablespoons
1 × 15ml spoon/ 1 tablespoon	Chinese rice wine or dry sherry	1 tablespoon
1 × 5ml spoon/ 1 teaspoon	sugar	1 teaspoon
1 × 15ml spoon/ 1 tablespoon	cornflour (cornstarch)	1 tablespoon
225g/8 oz	lean minced (ground) pork	½ lb
	4 water chestnuts, chopped	
	salt	
2 × 15ml spoons/ 2 tablespoons	oil	2 tablespoons
	sprigs parsley	

Soak the dried mushrooms in warm water for 15–30 minutes, until swollen. Drain in a sieve, reserving the water. Cut off and discard any stalks. To make the stuffing, mix together 1 × 15ml spoon/1 tablespoon of the soy sauce, the rice wine or sherry, sugar and cornflour (cornstarch). Stir in the pork and water chestnuts, and season with salt.

Heat the oil in a large frying pan. Place the mushrooms in the pan, rounded side downwards. Divide the stuffing between them and spread it flat with a knife. Fry the mushrooms over a moderate heat for 1 minute, until the undersides are slightly browned. Pour 4 × 15ml spoons/ 4 tablespoons of the reserved soaking water into the pan, bring to the boil, cover the pan, and stew for 15 minutes over a very low heat.

Remove the mushrooms carefully from the pan with a slotted spoon, and arrange on a warmed dish, stuffing side up. Add the remaining soy sauce to the pan and re-heat the liquid, stirring. Pour the sauce over the mushrooms, garnish with the parsley and serve.

Note If you cannot get dried Chinese mushrooms, use large, flat, fresh mushrooms.

Chinese Stuffed Mushrooms

Metric/imperial		American
	8 dried Chinese mushrooms	
100g/4 oz	lean pork, shredded	$\frac{1}{4}$ lb
1 × 15ml spoon/ 1 tablespoon	chopped onion	1 tablespoon
	1 small piece root ginger, finely chopped	
1 × 15ml spoon/ 1 tablespoon	bamboo shoots or water chestnuts, finely chopped	1 tablespoon
1½ × 5ml spoons/ 1½ teaspoons	soy sauce	1½ teaspoons
1½ × 5ml spoons/ 1½ teaspoons	Chinese rice wine or dry sherry	1½ teaspoons
1 × 2.5ml spoon/ ½ teaspoon	oil	½ teaspoon
1 × 15ml spoon/ 1 tablespoon	chopped parsley	1 tablespoon

Make sure the mushrooms are large and unbroken. Soak the mushrooms in hot water for 15–30 minutes, until swollen. Drain well and remove the stalks. Mix together the pork, onion, ginger, bamboo shoots or water chestnuts, soy sauce, rice wine or sherry and oil. Fill the mushroom caps with this mixture, pressing down firmly. Place them close together on a flat dish or dinner plate, cover loosely with a sheet of aluminium foil, and steam for 30 minutes, with the lid on. Transfer to a warm dish, sprinkle with the parsley and serve as an hors d'oeuvre to a Chinese meal.
Note If you cannot get dried Chinese mushrooms, use large, flat, fresh mushrooms.

Leeks in Batter

Metric/imperial		American
	8 thin leeks	
1 × 15ml spoon/ 1 tablespoon	oil	1 tablespoon
2 × 15ml spoons/ 2 tablespoons	soy sauce	2 tablespoons
1 × 15ml spoon/ 1 tablespoon	lemon juice	1 tablespoon
	salt, pepper, grated nutmeg	
	sugar	
	flour for coating	
	1 egg	
	oil for deep frying	

Remove all green parts from the leeks and wash thoroughly in cold water. Drain and cut diagonally across into pieces 5–7.5cm/2–3 inches long. Bring a pan of salted water to the boil, and stir in the oil. Add the pieces of leek. Cover the pan, reduce the heat and simmer until the leeks are tender (about 10 minutes).

Meanwhile mix together the soy sauce and lemon juice. Season with salt, pepper and a pinch of sugar. Put the sauce into a jug.

Put the flour on a plate. Break the egg into a bowl and beat it. Remove the leeks from the pan, drain and season with grated nutmeg. Roll in the flour, dip in the egg, and deep fry for 2 minutes, until crisp and golden-brown. Remove and drain on absorbent paper, place on a warmed dish and serve at once. Hand the sauce separately.

Bamboo Shoot Salad

Metric/imperial		American
	1 clove garlic	
	salt, ground ginger	
2 × 15ml spoons/ 2 tablespoons	soy sauce	2 tablespoons
3 × 15ml spoons/ 3 tablespoons	vinegar	3 tablespoons
2 × 15ml spoons/ 2 tablespoons	oil	2 tablespoons
	2 hard-boiled eggs, chopped	
	1 red pepper, de-seeded and chopped	
	sugar	
225g/8 oz	canned bamboo shoots, drained and sliced	½ lb
75g/3 oz	sweet pickled cucumber, sliced	½ cup
	¼ cooked celeriac root	
1 × 15ml spoon/ 1 tablespoon	chopped tarragon	1 tablespoon
1 × 15ml spoon/ 1 tablespoon	chopped dill	1 tablespoon

Crush the garlic with salt. Stir together a pinch of ground ginger, the soy sauce, vinegar and oil to make a smooth dressing. Mix together the eggs and pepper, season with salt and sugar, then mix with the dressing and stand in the refrigerator for 20 minutes. Mix together the bamboo shoots, cucumber and celeriac. Pour the chilled dressing over the vegetables and mix carefully. Garnish with the chopped herbs and serve.

Bamboo Shoot Salad

Chinese Spring Onion (Scallion) Tassels

spring onions (scallions), as required	

These decorations are always made from spring onions (scallions), even though they are sometimes referred to as shallot tassels. In Chinese cooking they are used as an edible garnish with many dishes.

Trim off the root as closely as possible. Cut away all except 7.5cm/3 inches of the green stem. With a very sharp knife, cut down the green stem to a depth of 2–2.5cm/ ¾–1 inch, and then make a second cut at right angles to it. Bend the four strips out slightly. Place the onions in a bowl of iced water, containing a few ice cubes, until the ends curl over. The same effect can be obtained by moistening the onions, and then putting them in the freezer compartment of a refrigerator, again just until the ends curl over.

DESSERTS

Lychees

Lychees, popular as they are in Europe, originally come from China. The fruits are almost round, have a scaly red skin, and grow in clusters on trees about 9m/30 feet high. They have been popular in China since ancient times. Their flesh is firm and white and their flavour is slightly reminiscent of cherries, with a touch of nutmeg. Nowadays, canned lychees are available in oriental food shops and are on the menu of every Chinese restaurant.

Today, lychees are also grown in South Africa, India, Australia, Hawaii, Brazil and Florida, Hong Kong is the main source of canned lychees, these are preserved in syrup. The Chinese almost always eat the fruit cooked, or dried, hence another name for the lychee is Chinese hazelnut. Lychees are also a rich source of Vitamin C.

Lychees

Chinese Honey Apples

Metric/imperial		American
	2 eggs	
100g/4 oz	flour	1 cup
150ml/¼ pint	water	⅔ cup
	pinch of salt	
	4 dessert apples, peeled	
50ml/2 fl oz	oil	¼ cup
100g/4 oz	honey	⅓ cup
50ml/1 fl oz	groundnut (peanut) oil	¼ cup

To make the batter, mix together the eggs, flour, water and a pinch of salt in a bowl. Remove the apple cores with an apple corer; cut the apples into thick rounds. Heat the first quantity of oil in a frying pan. Dip the apple rings into the batter, then fry them in the hot oil for 3 minutes each side, until golden brown. Heat the honey and groundnut (peanut) oil in a pan. Dip the fried apple rings in this mixture and allow to cool.

Note In China, a bowl of water with ice cubes in it is served with this dessert. The freshly fried apple rings are speared on chopsticks and dipped into the water so that the honey crystallizes.

Peking Pears

Metric/imperial		American
	4 ripe pears, peeled	
4 × 15ml spoons/ 4 tablespoons	honey	4 tablespoons
50g/2 oz	chopped walnuts	½ cup
1 × 5ml spoon/ 1 teaspoon	lemon juice	1 teaspoon
	ground ginger	

Remove the cores from the pears with an apple corer. Mix together in a bowl the honey, walnuts, lemon juice and a small pinch of ginger. Put this stuffing inside the pears. Grease an ovenproof dish and set the pears upright in it. Cover the dish, place on the bottom shelf of the oven and bake for 40 minutes at 200°C/400°F/Gas 6. Remove the lid from the dish 10 minutes before the end of the cooking time. Serve at once.

Korean Caramelized Bananas

Metric/imperial		American
	4 bananas, peeled	
20g/¾ oz	cornflour (cornstarch)	3 tablespoons
	2 egg whites, beaten	
	flour for coating	
	oil for deep frying	
15g/½ oz	butter	1 tablespoon
100g/4 oz	sugar	½ cup
2 × 15ml spoons/ 2 tablespoons	water	2 tablespoons
25g/1 oz	sesame seeds	3 tablespoons

Cut the bananas into pieces 2cm/¾inch long. Mix the cornflour (cornstarch) into the egg whites. Sprinkle some flour on a plate. Dip the banana pieces first in the flour, then in the egg white mixture, and deep fry them until golden brown. Remove and drain on absorbent paper.

To make the sauce, gently heat the butter and sugar in a pan until golden brown. Stir in the water and sesame seeds. Add the fried banana pieces and turn carefully in the sauce. Transfer to a warmed and greased dish and serve.

Peking Dust

Metric/imperial		American
450g/1 lb	unsweetened chestnut purée	1 lb
150ml/¼ pint	water	⅔ cup
500ml/17 fl oz	whipping cream	1 pint
3 × 15ml spoons/ 3 tablespoons	caster (superfine) sugar	3 tablespoons
1 × 5ml spoon/ 1 teaspoon	vanilla sugar	1 teaspoon
1 × 15ml spoon/ 1 tablespoon	soft dark brown sugar	1 tablespoon
100g/4 oz	granulated sugar	½ cup
	mandarin orange segments, blanched almonds, walnuts, and glacé (candied) cherries to decorate	

Mix together in a bowl the chestnut purée and 80ml/3 fl oz/6 US tablespoons of the water. Put the cream in another bowl and beat until it begins to thicken. Add the caster (superfine) and vanilla sugars and beat the cream until stiff. Remove half of the cream from the bowl and blend it into the chestnut purée mixture with the brown sugar. Bring the remaining water and the granulated sugar to the boil in a pan. Boil, stirring constantly, until a thick syrup is formed.

Dip the fruits and nuts (use as many as or as few as you wish) into this syrup, and then leave them to cool and harden on a piece of greaseproof (waxed) paper. Put the chestnut purée mixture in an icing bag. Using a nozzle with a small, plain, round opening, squeeze the mixture out in small lengths and heap them up on a dish. Cover with the remaining whipped cream and decorate with the glazed fruits and nuts.

Korean Caramelized Bananas

INDEX